Passages

EXPLORING THE BIBLE IN FOUR MOVEMENTS

An Exhibition Guide

Jennifer Atwood and Stacey L. Douglas

Editors

museum of the Bible

"Passages" is a traveling exhibition of Museum of the Bible

Passages: Exploring the Bible in Four Movements–An Exhibition Guide
Content and item diagnostics created by the curators of the Museum of the Bible:
Lance B. Allred, Jennifer J. Atwood, Norman C. Conrad, Josephine K. Dru,
Herschel A. Hepler, Heather N. Reichstadt, and Amy Van Dyke

Edited by
Jennifer Atwood, Curator of Medieval Manuscripts and
Stacey L. Douglas, Writer and Editor, Museum of the Bible

Cover design by Richelle D. McKinley
Cover image shows detail of King David from the copy of
an illustrated Book of Hours printed by Simon Vostre around 1512
which King Henry VIII of England gave as a gift to his cousin
(The Green Collection)

Layout and design by Allentown Digital Services, RR Donnelley

Prepared for
Passages
26565 Bouquet Canyon Road
Santa Clarita, California 91350
April 3, 2015-Febraury 27, 2016
www.ExplorePassages.com

Published by
Museum of the Bible
7707 SW 44th Street
Oklahoma City, OK 73179
405.745.1750
www.museumoftheBible.org

© Museum of the Bible, 2015

All rights reserved
No part of this publication may be reproduced in any form
without written permission from Museum of the Bible

ISBN 978-1-943082-00-1

PRINTED IN THE UNITED STATES OF AMERICA

Table of Contents

PRELUDE	*1*
OVERTURE	*3*
MOVEMENT 1—TRANSMISSION	*5*
Cuneiform: The Birth of Writing	*7*
The Dead Sea Scroll from the Caves at Qumran	*9*
Medieval Scribes: From Monks to Urban Professionals	*13*
The Gutenberg Press and the Advent of Printing	*17*
The Tent of Discovery and the Cairo Genizah	*22*
The Lunar Bible: The First Book on the Moon	*28*
The Bible in the Digital Age	*31*
The Bible—There's an App for That (Interactive Display)	*31*
Using Augmented Reality to Bring the Bible to Life (Interactive Displays)	*32*
MOVEMENT 2—CONTROVERSY	*35*
The Biblical Canon: A Collection of Collections	*37*
The Reformation Theatre (Video)	*42*
The Bible and Slavery	*46*
Jewish Persecution: Pre-Holocaust Pogroms	*53*
The Holocaust and Kristallnacht	*55*
MOVEMENT 3—TRANSLATION	*63*
Jerome's Cave	*65*
Early Translations of the Bible	*65*
Medieval European Translations and Conversation in a Peasants' Village (Video)	*68*
Non-European Translations of the Bible	*71*
The Contribution of William Tyndale	*73*
John Knox and Reformation Translations	*74*
The King James Bible: A Translation to Unite the English	*78*
Bible Translation in the Modern Era	*82*

MOVEMENT 4—IMPACT	*87*
The Bible and Jewish Liturgy	*89*
The Bible and Christian Liturgy	*94*
LITURGICAL SIGNIFICANCE EXPLORED	*97*
Adornment of and Art about the Bible	*101*
ARTISTIC TECHNIQUES EXPLORED	*108*
"The Battle Hymn of the Republic"	*108*
Impact Theater—"Book of Books" (Video)	*113*
REPRISE	*115*
About Museum of the Bible	*117*
By the Numbers	*117*
Museum Timeline	*118*
What Others Are Saying	*118*

Prelude

Music moves and flows. Dissonance turns into harmony. Solo instruments prepare us for the symphonic wave of a full orchestra. So it is with the reception of the Bible.

In this exhibition, we invite you to follow the history of both the Jewish and the Christian Bible as they move and flow through time, creating dissonance and harmony, impacting the lives of individuals and societies.

One of the stories attributed to Jesus of Nazareth is the story of a man who went out into the field to sow. Some seeds fall on fertile ground, others between thorns, some fall on the road, and others are eaten by birds. Our hope is that our effort to introduce you to the Book of Books through selected rare books and artifacts will open your ears and hearts for the stories they tell.

And may the seed fall on fertile ground.

Dr. David Trobisch
Director of the Green Collection
The Feast of Saint Patrick, 2015

OVERTURE

Passages: The Bible in Four Movements is structured around four themes that interweave and play off one another in the history of the Bible:

- Transmission
- Controversy
- Translation
- Impact

While these themes have their own unique story, elements and motifs from each are easily found among the others.

Transmission follows various moments and movements of the Bible's dissemination, not only through time but also through various communities. From the beginnings of writing to the digital age, the history of how new information—including the Bible—has been produced and delivered involves the development of a vast array of communication media. Indeed, history shows how various faith communities have often been "early adopters" of new media, eager to make the Bible and its message accessible in new and meaningful ways.

Controversy explores points of difficulty and tension, including the more jarring and discordant passages, in the Bible's development and history. Uncomfortable matters confront us when considering the composition and development of the biblical canon, since the voices of various communities have the potential to sound out of tune with one another in the midst of both agreement and diversity. Furthermore, there are also those who would stifle, silence, or snuff out not only the Bible as a book, but those whose understanding of the book conflicts, even contradicts, their own use of it.

Translation occurs in the process of transmission and is sometimes fueled by controversy. Bible translators regularly face and overcome numerous challenges in moving from one language to another: safeguarding accuracy in translation, delivering meaningful renderings of the biblical text to a wide range of readers, facing political or religious opposition, and even developing literary language systems for communities whose language has been oral rather than written. Still, translators strive to be both accurate and effective in rendering the ancient biblical texts, even if their translations are is not perfect or accepted by all.

Finally, *Impact* traces and follows several lines of movement, and we see—and hear—points of impact in the midst of transmission, translation, and controversy. Wherever the Bible has gone, it has unavoidably had an impact, both in Jewish and Christian faith communities, but also in wider cultures. Law, art, literature, music, theater, science, and philosophy—not to mention too many geographical places and cities to name—tell of the influence and impact of the Bible.

These four themes presented for the *Passages* exhibition in Santa Clarita, CA, help show something of the dynamics and movements in the Bible's history that have played through time and continue in the present.

Movement 1—Transmission

Textual transmission refers to the ways in which ideas spread using a written form. For roughly the first 4,500 years after writing developed, this primarily involved copying texts by hand. With Johannes Gutenberg's invention of movable type for the printing press around AD 1450, printed works became easier and faster to produce and, thus, more readily available. More recently, the invention and ongoing developments of digital technologies in the twentieth and twenty-first centuries have revolutionized the way we interact with words, texts, and information.

The Bible is the most widely disseminated text of all time. World leaders throughout history, from Constantine to Charlemagne, have championed the transmission of the Bible, and it has been at the forefront of many of the most important technological advancements involving the written word for the last 2,000 years. This section explores the process of textual transmission as it has impacted and been impacted by the Bible.

Cuneiform: The Birth of Writing

Cuneiform (Latin for "wedge-shaped") represents the world's earliest known writing system, and first appeared in southern Iraq around 3200 BC. The oldest cuneiform tablets come from the ancient city of Uruk (the biblical Erech of Genesis 10) in the temple precinct of the Babylonian goddess Inanna. It was initially used as a means of recording temple property—including livestock and slaves—as well as the temple's agricultural output, or the production of beer and bread.

The system of using a reed stylus to impress wedges into a wet clay tablet emerged from earlier methods of recordkeeping that involved using small clay tokens to record things like the number of animals in a herd. These tokens were sometimes stored in hollow clay spheres, or bullae. To easily recall what was inside the bullae, the tokens were sometimes impressed on the outside of the clay. Towards the end of the fourth millennium BC, Mesopotamians dispensed with the use of tokens and bullae altogether, instead smashing the clay flat for use as a writing surface. Through these humble beginnings, a revolution began in how individuals communicated.

Like the Roman alphabet, cuneiform is a system of writing and not a language. The first language cuneiform recorded was Sumerian, the language of the land of Sumer in southern Iraq (probably the land of Shinar referenced in Genesis 10 and 11). Sumerian died out as a spoken language in about 2000 BC, but the cuneiform writing system was borrowed and used by the speakers of other languages, including Akkadian, a Semitic language, and Hittite, an Indo-European language. Cuneiform tablets have been found at sites ranging from Egypt to Turkey and Israel to Iran, and was in use even as late as the first century AD.

Scribal Training   [Case 0100]

Within a few hundred years of its development, cuneiform writing had spread throughout much of southern Iraq. It began to see use beyond just recordkeeping and administration, such as celebrating royal achievements, composing correspondence for personal business, and political communications. It was also used to compose hymns that celebrated and venerated the gods.

With these developments, there quickly arose a class of scribes—usually boys from elite families–trained in the art of reading and writing. This case contains some examples of how scribes learned their art. For instance, early scribal training consisted of a schoolmaster inscribing several lines of vocabulary on a lentil-shaped piece of clay (Items 0101, 0102), which the student was to copy on the reverse. More advanced students copied longer sections of standardized lists of related words and phrases. In the examples here (Items 0103, 0104, 0105), the schoolmaster wrote a list on the left half of the tablet. The student then copied the words on the right half. After copying, he scraped off a thin layer of clay and re-wrote the list again—like a student today with a dry erase board. Usually, the student continued copying until he had completely scraped off his side of the tablet down to nothing, as is the case in these examples.

After completing their training, many scribes went on to work for temples and palaces in an administrative capacity. As a result, it was important for scribes to be accomplished not only in reading and writing, but also in math and accounting. Item 0106 represents one student's efforts at writing out the nines multiplication table. Unfortunately, he made an error and mistakenly answered 9 x 6 as 49 rather than 54!

Case 0100 – Item Diagnostics

0101:	**CUNEIFORM LENTIL** Scribal exercise Clay Southern Iraq Circa 1800 BC GC.CUN.000245	0104:	**LEXICAL LIST** Advanced scribal exercise Clay Southern Iraq Circa 1800 BC GC.CUN.000185
0102:	**CUNEIFORM LENTIL** Scribal exercise with lines 318, 317, and 319 of Hh VIII concerning reed mats Clay Southern Iraq Circa 1800 BC GC.CUN.000246	0105:	**LEXICAL LIST** Advanced scribal exercise with EN-words Clay Southern Iraq Circa 1800 BC GC.CUN.000248
0103:	**LEXICAL LIST** Advanced scribal exercise Clay Southern Iraq Circa 1800 BC GC.CUN.000247	0106:	**MULTIPLICATION TABLET** Multiplication table by 9s Clay Southern Iraq Circa 1800 BC GC.CUN.000249

Transmission of Information and Ideology   [Case 0200]

Mesopotamian kings often contended with others to expand their territorial holdings. Success meant increased access to agricultural holdings, as well as control of canals for irrigation, communication, and transportation. The large clay slab here (Item 0201) represents an unnamed king's efforts to delineate the borders of the ancient city-state of Umma, located in far southern Mesopotamia. Scholars have recovered a number of documents that show ongoing conflict over the border between Umma and Lagash, its neighbor to the south. Those documents, however, have largely been written from the point of view of Lagash. This tablet, from Umma, provides historians with a different viewpoint on the conflict.

One of the major tasks of any Mesopotamian ruler was the construction and maintenance of temples and other buildings dedicated to local or national gods. To commemorate such acts, the king often had scribes write inscriptions on a clay cone or nail. These were then inserted into the plaster walls of the temple, exposing only their heads, which were often painted to create a mosaic of triangles or other geometric shapes. The two clay nails here (Items 0202, 0203) were commissioned by Gudea, the local ruler of Lagash. Kings also venerated the gods by commissioning hymns celebrating the god's greatness—and the king's piety. Item 0204 is a fragment of a hymn to the chief god of the Sumerian pantheon, Enlil.

Writing was not just used by the king, however. Individuals sometimes used writing to communicate with others over long distances. Such letters typically updated a relative or business partner on family matters and business happenings. In contrast to royal compositions, letters such as Item 0205 often reveal much about daily life of average Mesopotamians.

The Dead Sea Scrolls from the Caves at Qumran

In the late 1940s, three Bedouin shepherds grazing their flocks on the northwest shores of the Dead Sea found a cave containing several ancient jars. One jar housed three Hebrew scrolls, including a mostly complete copy of Isaiah. Before this discovery, the oldest known Hebrew manuscript of this text was the Aleppo Codex from the early tenth century AD. The discovery in these jars predated this manuscript by over one thousand years.

Case 0200 – Item Diagnostics

0201:	**BORDERS OF SHARA CUNEIFORM TABLET** Royal inscription of Ĝiša-kidu on large tablet, RIME 1.12.6.2 Clay Southern Iraq Circa 2500 BC GC.CUN.000179
0202:	**GUDEA CONE** Royal inscription on cone, RIME 3/1.1.7.37 Clay Southern Iraq Circa 2130 BC GC.CUN.000241
0203:	**GUDEA CONE** Royal inscription on cone, RIME 3/1.1.7.48 Clay Southern Iraq Circa 2130 BC GC.CUN.000251
0204:	**HYMN TO ENLIL** Enlil A, lines 65-75 Clay Southern Iraq Circa 1900 BC GC.CUN.000240
0205:	**OLD BABYLONIAN LETTER** Letter on tablet Clay Southern Iraq Circa 1800 BC GC.CUN.000215

Over the following decade, researchers and Bedouins scoured the surrounding area and found thousands of textual fragments in ten other caves. Physical evidence associated these caves with an ancient settlement at a nearby site called Khirbet Qumran. It was occupied from the mid-third century BC until around AD 70 by a Jewish group that left Jerusalem, most likely because they believed the priesthood and other varieties of Judaism had become corrupt. In addition to numerous copies of the Hebrew Bible, this community produced and studied many commentaries and other texts based on the biblical texts.

The present room is modeled on Cave 4, one of the most famous caves at Qumran, which yielded more fragments of biblical texts than any of the others. This cave had been used to store thousands of texts, much like a library. When it was rediscovered in the early 1950s, the wooden shelves that once lined its walls had long since disintegrated, and researchers found the floor strewn with texts.

Along the walls here you can examine exact replicas of the three scrolls first discovered in the jar from Cave 1 (Cases 0300, 0400, and 0600) and of three fragmentary originals found in Cave 4 (Case 0500). In the final case, you see actual fragments from the Dead Sea Scrolls (Case 0700).

The Great Isaiah Scroll   [Case 0300]

The first biblical manuscript found at Qumran, the Great Isaiah Scroll (known as 1QIsa[a]), was also the most fully preserved. The original resides in the Shrine of the Book at the Israel Museum in Jerusalem. The facsimile displayed here—an exact copy of the original scroll, even reproducing the details of the original hand-stitching and damage patterns—is based on photos taken in Jerusalem in 1948 by American researchers John Trever and William Brownlee not long after the Cave 1 discoveries. Measuring 7.34 meters (24 feet) long, 1QIsa[a] clearly illustrates why most individual books of the Hebrew Bible at that time were copied on separate scrolls. Fitting even several of the longer prophetic books together on a single scroll—much less all of the Hebrew Bible—would have been physically unmanageable.

Case 0300 – Item Diagnostics

0301:	GREAT ISAIAH SCROLL (1QISA^A) FACSIMILE
	Hebrew, Ink on Parchment
	Qumran, Cave 1
	2nd century BC
	GC.FAC.000123.1

Prior to the Qumran discoveries, modern translations of Isaiah from Hebrew were based on the oldest Masoretic Text (MT) manuscripts dated to the tenth and eleventh centuries AD. Comparing 1QIsa^a with those manuscripts demonstrates a remarkable degree of consistency between these copies made more than a thousand years apart, with close matches in content, sequence, and divisions throughout most of this very long book.

One significant physical difference is that 1QIsa^a was written without the vowel markings ("pointing") that appear in later manuscripts. The absence of vowel points in this and other early Hebrew manuscripts means certain words are ambiguous and can potentially be interpreted in more than one way, depending on which vowels are read. Recognizing this fact is quite important for understanding the history of biblical transmission in that period.

Occasionally, other differences also occur. For example, in column II, 1QIsa^a goes straight from 2:9a to 2:11 without the text that usually appears in between (2:9b-10). However, other copies of Isaiah from Qumran do include the intervening text. A more visible example appears at Isaiah 40:7b in column XXXIII, where a second scribe has inserted in line seven the phrase: "When the breath of •••• [YHWH] blows upon it" using four dots to write the divine name. In contrast, the original scribe uses normal letters for the divine name.

The overall combination of similarities and differences makes the Great Isaiah Scroll both a supporting witness for the MT. They show how faithfully it was copied between circa 100 BC–AD 900, and as an independent witness—together with other copies of Isaiah found at Qumran—that improves our understanding of what Hebrew copies of this prophetic book looked like during the first and second centuries BC.

The Community Rule   [Case 0400]

The caves at Qumran included several copies of a text known as the Community Rule (1QS), or Manual of Discipline, based on its ancient Hebrew title, *Serekh haYahad*. The facsimile of the scroll shown here is the most complete copy of this text. Of the seven scrolls discovered in Cave 1, this was among the first three found preserved in a jar. The original resides in the Shrine of the Book at the Israel Museum in Jerusalem.

Case 0400 – Item Diagnostics

0401:	COMMUNITY RULE (1QS), FACSIMILE
	Ink on parchment
	Qumran, Cave 1
	Early 1st century BC
	GC.FAC.000123.2

This text provides valuable information about the motivations, beliefs, and lifestyle of the Jews who preserved the Dead Sea Scrolls. Column V explains its purpose: "This is the rule (*serekh*) for the men of the Community who freely volunteer to convert from all evil and to keep themselves steadfast in all he [God] commanded in compliance with his will.…These are the regulations for their behavior… when they are enrolled in the Community."

Two passages in this document are of particular interest for the history of Bible transmission. Column VI gives us a glimpse of how the Jews at Qumran continually incorporated the Bible into their communal life:

"In the place where the Ten assemble, there should not be missing a man to interpret the Law, day and night, always with one relieving another. And the Many shall be on watch together for a third of each night of the year in order to read the book, explain the regulation, and bless together."

Column VIII explains *why* this community had withdrawn to the desert by quoting an excerpt from Isaiah 40:3:

"They are to be separated from... the dwelling of the men of sin, to go to the wilderness in order to open his way there, as it is written:

'In the wilderness prepare the way of •••• [YHWH], make straight in the desert a highway for our God.'"

The passage explains that the way the Jews at Qumran will "open the way" for God is by obeying the Hebrew sacred text: "This is the study of the Law which he commanded through... Moses, in order to act in compliance with all that has been revealed... and according to what the prophets have revealed through his holy spirit."

Three Biblical Fragments from Cave 4   [Case 0500]

The items shown in this case offer a small sampling of how the texts from Qumran improve modern understanding of which books were preserved and studied as sacred scripture during the late Second Temple period. There are two basic types of evidence: which books were copied, and which were quoted in other texts as being authoritative.

Case 0500 – Item Diagnostics

0501:	PESHER ISAIAH^B (4Q162), FACSIMILE
	Ink on parchment
	Qumran, Cave 4
	Latter half of 1st century BC
	GC.FAC.000123.8
0502:	FRAGMENTS FROM QOHELETH (4Q109), FACSIMILE
	Ink on parchment
	Qumran, Cave 4
	Latter half of 1st century BC
	GC.FAC.000123.5-.7
0503:	TESTIMONIA (4Q175), FACSIMILE
	Ink on parchment
	Qumran, Cave 4
	Mid-1st century BC
	GC.FAC.000123.9

Before the destruction of the Second Temple in AD 70, there were two sets of books from today's Hebrew Bible, or Tanakh (TNK), that were recognized as canonical groupings: the Law (*Torah*) and the Prophets (*Nevi'im*). Fragments from every book in both groups have been found at Qumran (see Case 0700). The fragments here from Ecclesiastes (Item 0502), belong to a third group, later labeled the Writings (*Ketuvim*). The discoveries at Qumran indicate that all but one of the individual books among the Writings—which include Psalms, Proverbs, Job, Song of Songs, Ruth, Lamentations, Ecclesiastes, Daniel, Ezra, Nehemiah, and Chronicles—were treated as scripture by this desert community. Only Esther has yet to be found. This may mean that the book was not transmitted by this community, or it may just mean that no copies have survived. For example, over fifty years after the initial discoveries, there was no trace of the Book of Nehemiah either, but within the past decade, two fragments of it have been clearly identified.

The other fragments in this case demonstrate two kinds of biblical interpretation at Qumran. A *pesher*

(Hebrew for interpretive "solution") is a commentary on successive quotations from a single book. The Pesher of Isaiahᴮ (4Q162) applies quotes from Isaiah 5 to the Qumran community's situation (Item 0501). Another type of commentary presents excerpts from multiple books to explore a common theme. The Testimonia (4Q175) quotes two passages from Deuteronomy about Moses as the original prophet, followed by two Messianic quotations from Numbers 24:15-17 and Deuteronomy 33:8-11 (Item 0503). The interpretive text puts all of these quotations in the context of a series of psalms attributed to Joshua, and quotes Joshua 6:26 as another prophecy.

These three facsimiles reproduce originals from the National Archaeological Museum in Amman, Jordan. All were found in Cave 4.

A Commentary on Habakkuk   [Case 0600]

The term *pesher* (plural *pesharim*) is Hebrew for interpretive "solution". It is the modern label for a certain type of biblical commentary from Qumran, which frequently uses this term to signal a shift from quotation to interpretation.

The facsimile commentary to Habakkuk (1QpHab) shown here (Item 0601) is the most fully preserved of approximately fifteen examples of *pesharim* found among the Dead Sea Scrolls. A more fragmentary example, from Isaiah, appears in Case 0500. Like the Great Isaiah Scroll (Case 0300) and 1QS (Case 0400), the original scroll containing this commentary on Habakkuk was found in a jar in Cave 1 and now resides in the Shrine of the Book at the Israel Museum in Jerusalem.

Case 0600 – Item Diagnostics

0601:	PESHER HABAKKUK (1QPHAB), FACSIMILE
	Ink on parchment
	Qumran, Cave 1
	Latter half of 1st century BC
	GC.FAC.000123.3-.4

Visually, this scroll exhibits two interesting scribal features: visible ruling, which helped scribes maintain consistent spacing between lines and a consistent line width across each column as they copied the text by hand, and the use of paleo-Hebrew—an older form of the Hebrew alphabet—to write the divine name. Also known as the "Tetragrammaton," the divine name consists of the four consonants YHWH. It looks something like this—𐤉𐤄𐤅𐤄. See if you can find it in column VI, next to last line; column X, lines 7 and 14; and column XI, line 10.

This scroll provides both a significant window into the Qumran community and an example of how the Jewish authors of the New Testament might have interpreted Habakkuk and other prophetic texts.

Ancient Fragments of the Law and the Prophets   [Case 0700]

The three items shown in this case illustrate how a majority of texts found among the Dead Sea Scrolls survive as small fragments. Each preserves only a few lines often with substantial parts of each line missing. Why then are the Qumran discoveries regarded as such an important contribution to the history of biblical transmission?

First, it is possible to learn a surprising amount from a small piece such as the ones shown here. Similar to a skilled detective reconstructing significant facts from seemingly insignificant clues, scholars can learn a lot about the missing text and the circumstances of a manuscript's creation from the details present in these small fragments, like ink composition, features of the writing surface, writing style, spelling practices, textual content, and more.

Second, the information contained within each fragment contributes to the bigger picture of what the Hebrew Bible looked like during these pivotal centuries. These texts were written shortly after the first Greek translations of the Jewish Scriptures, before the rise of the codex, before specific discussions about the Hebrew canon, and before the creation of the New Testament.

The three fragments here represent two of the three major divisions that would come to be known as the Tanakh (**TNK**).

T stands for *Torah*, meaning "Law," or the five "books of Moses"—Genesis (Item 0701), Exodus, Leviticus, Numbers, and Deuteronomy.

N, is for *Nevi'im* or "Prophets," with two major groupings: (1) the Former Prophets, consisting of books that narrate the early history of Israel as a nation—Joshua, Judges, Samuel, and Kings—and (2) the Latter Prophets. The Latter Prophets were subdivided into two groups: the three Major Prophets (Item 0702)—Isaiah, Jeremiah, and Ezekiel—and the twelve Minor Prophets (Item 0703)—Hosea through Malachi. The terms "Major" and "Minor" (which did not arise until centuries later) referred to length rather than importance. Each of the "Major" prophets was so long it needed an entire scroll (as shown in Case 0300). The twelve "Minor" prophets were short enough to fit together on a single scroll.

The third division in the Tanakh—**K** for *Ketuvim* or "Writings"—is discussed in Case 0500.

Case 0700 – Item Diagnostics

	First Rotation: April-September		**Second Rotation: October-Closing**
0701:	GENESIS 32, DEAD SEA SCROLLS FRAGMENT, FACSIMILE Ink on parchment Qumran, possibly Cave 4 Early to mid-1st century BC Reproduction of GC.SCR.000124	0701:	GENESIS 32, DEAD SEA SCROLLS FRAGMENT Ink on parchment Qumran, possibly Cave 4 Early to mid-1st century BC GC.SCR.000124
0702:	JEREMIAH 23, DEAD SEA SCROLLS FRAGMENT Ink on parchment Qumran, possibly Cave 4 Mid-1st century BC GC.SCR.003172	0702:	EZEKIEL 28, DEAD SEA SCROLLS FRAGMENT Ink on parchment Qumran, possibly Cave 4 Latter half of 1st century BC GC.SCR.0003174
0703:	JONAH 4, DEAD SEA SCROLLS FRAGMENT Ink on parchment Qumran, possibly Cave 4 Late 1st century BC GC.SCR.003171	0703:	MICAH 1, DEAD SEA SCROLLS FRAGMENT Ink on parchment Qumran, possibly Cave 4 Late 1st century BC to early 1st century AD GC.SCR.0003183

Medieval Scribes: From Monks to Urban Professionals

Scribes are people trained in the craft of copying, composing, and recording texts by hand. They have existed in almost every literate society since writing began. For over two thousand years, the texts of the Bible were preserved and passed on primarily through their work. Before the birth of Christianity, scribes in the Mediterranean world usually wrote on clay tablets, as shown by cuneiform texts from Mesopotamia, or on rolls, like the Dead Sea Scrolls found at Qumran.

A new technology that developed during the early centuries of the Church was the codex, which we know today as the book. Arranged by stacking sheets into folded piles, sewing the piles together, and writing on both sides of each sheet, the codex allowed scribes to fit more writing together than the roll. The codex also made it easier to flip between different sections of the text and compare texts between authors.

Although the codex was not invented by Christians, its widespread use was closely intertwined with the spread of Christianity. Initially the new format was used to bind multiple compositions together, such as the four Gospels or all of the Pauline letters, into a single, travel-friendly unit. Eventually this development led to the mass production—still copied by hand—of the entire Bible in one volume. With rare exceptions, codices also replaced scrolls as the format used for transmitting other literature.

The term "manuscript" literally means "hand-written," from the Latin words *manus* ("hand") and *scriptum* ("written"). While that description also applies to tablets and rolls, both of which were copied by hand, "manuscript" has essentially come to mean "hand-written codex."

Christian Scribes in Egypt and the Greek East   [Case 0800]

Greek was the first written language of the early Church. Although Christianity was born within the Roman Empire, the sacred Hebrew texts it inherited from its Jewish roots had been translated into Greek centuries earlier, and all of the early Christian authors whose writings would become the New Testament wrote in Greek rather than Latin, Hebrew, or Aramaic.

The manuscripts in this case represent a variety of Greek writing styles, from early majuscules—capital letters—in "informal round" (Item 0801) or "severe style" (Item 0802) to the lower-case minuscules that arose in later centuries (Item 0805). Most exhibit the scribal practice of *scriptio continua*, writing without regular spaces

Case 0800 – Item Diagnostics

0801:	LEAF FROM P. BODMER XXIV PSALMS 99-102 IN GREEK Ink on papyrus Egypt 3rd to 4th century AD GC.MS.000170.39	0804:	BIFOLIUM FROM THE CODEX CLIMACI RESCRIPTUS GOSPELS AND GOSPEL HARMONY MANUSCRIPT IN GREEK Reused for "The Ladder of Divine Ascent" in Syriac Ink on parchment Sinai, Egypt 7th–8th century AD and 9th century AD GC.MS.000149.55
0802:	THE "WYMAN FRAGMENT" ROMANS 4-5 IN GREEK Ink on parchment Egypt 3rd century AD GC.MS.000566	0805:	TWO FOLIOS FROM A FOUR-GOSPEL CODEX MATTHEW 19-20 IN BOULETÉE STYLE GREEK MINUSCULE Ink on parchment Probably Constantinople 10th century AD GC.MS.000376.1-.2
0803:	FACSIMILE OF BIFOLIUM FROM P. BODMER VIII 1 PETER 5 THROUGH 2 PETER 1 IN GREEK Ink on papyrus Egypt Late 3rd to early 4th century AD GC.FAC.000137.8	0806:	SCRIBAL INKWELL AND STYLUS Bronze Probably Levant Circa 5th to 8th century AD GC.OBJ.000150.1-.2

between words or even sentences. Since most manuscripts were copied to be read aloud, this visual continuity reflects the flow of spoken language. At the same time, scribes helped readers keep track of where they were in a codex by including section numbers and titles (Items 0801, 0805), page numbers (Item 0803), and book titles (Item 0803: "2nd Epistle of Peter").

A feature distinctive to Christian scribes across a wide range of time and geography is the way they abbreviated *nomina sacra*, "holy names" or "sacred nouns," by writing only the first and last letters with a horizontal line above them as a visual mark of respect. The four words most consistently treated this way were:

"Lord" - ⲕⲥ, ⲕⲛ, ⲕⲉ (Items 0801, 0804)
"God" - ⲑⲥ, ⲑⲩ (Items 0801, 0803)
"Christ" - ⲭⲡⲥ, ⲭⲩ/ⲭⲡⲩ (Items 0801, 0802, 0803)
"Jesus" - ⲓⲏⲥ/ⲓⲏ/ⲓⲥ, ⲓⲩ/ⲓⲏⲩ, ⲓⲛ (Items 0802, 0803, 0805)

This practice may be linked to the Jewish tradition of writing the divine name differently from its surrounding text; however, by including "Christ" and "Jesus" in the same category as "Lord" and "God," early Christian scribes may be reflecting a distinctive understanding of monotheism and messianism.

Before the advent of paper, Christian scribes used the two main types of writing material for Bible manuscripts: papyrus, made from the fibers of a reed-like plant grown in Egypt (Items 0801, 0803), and parchment, made from animal skin (Items 0802, 0804, 0805). The scribal practice of making palimpsests (from the Greek word for "rubbed smooth again") is seen in the pages from the Codex Climaci Rescriptus (Item 0804), where a centuries-old manuscript was washed and turned upside down to write a Syriac text on top.

Religious Scribes in the Latin West   [Case 0900]

In Europe during the early Middle Ages, most scribes were also Christian monks. Sixth-century monastic leaders like St. Cassiodorus and St. Benedict included in their monasteries libraries and *scriptoria*, or rooms set apart specifically for copying texts. These monasteries served as models for similar communities throughout Europe, and book production became a central part of monastic life. Medieval monks helped preserve not only the text of the Bible but also literary works by classical authors, such as Plato and Virgil.

Case 0900– Item Diagnostics

0901:	SAINT CECILIA BIBLE, VOLUME 2 Decorated manuscript on parchment Benedictine Abbey of Saint Cecilia Rome, Italy 2nd half of 11th century AD GC.MS.000229.2	0903:	CISTERCIAN OFFICE LECTIONARY FOR THE SUMMER SEASON Decorated manuscript on parchment Northern Italy, possibly Piacenza Circa 1260–1275 GC.MS.000772
0902:	BERNARD OF CLAIRVAUX, *SERMONS ON THE SONG OF SONGS* Decorated manuscript on parchment The Netherlands or Belgium Dated January 30, 1416 in scribal colophon GC.MS.000460	0904:	ROGERUS DE ERACLEA, *LENTEN "SCHOOL" SERMONS* Decorated manuscript on paper Tuscany, Italy Circa 1400–1410 GC.MS.000753

Most of the manuscripts in this case were copied in European *scriptoria* and were primarily produced for use within the monastic community. The single volume of a multi-volume Bible shown here (Item 0901) was copied in the monastic scriptorium at the Benedictine Abbey of Saint Cecilia in Rome. At least nine different scribes worked on this volume. Similarly, the lectionary here (Item 0903) was copied by scribes of the Cistercian Order. Cistercian scribes were the first to employ the *punctus circumflexus*, punctuation used to indicate breath marks. This was important because most of the reading that was taking place in a medieval monastery was done aloud, not only during religious services but also at mealtimes, meetings in the chapterhouse, and so on.

Later in the Middle Ages, a number of manuscripts were copied by educated individuals for their own personal use. Such is the case with the collection of sermons by Roger de Eraclea displayed here (Item 0904). This manuscript was likely copied by a Franciscan preacher for use as reference material when crafting his own sermons.

The Rise of the Professional Scribe   [Case 1000]

The first universities were founded in the middle of the twelfth century, and with them came the need for books to be available on a much larger scale than before. From then on, book production was primarily the work of professional urban scribes, who copied books not from religious motivations but for pay.

One of the most important developments in the history of the medieval Bible was the mass-production of the single-volume Bible (Item 1001). Before the thirteenth century, Latin Bibles were typically produced in multiple volumes. However, with the rise of universities in the 1200s, the one-volume format became standard for Bible

Case 1000– Item Diagnostics

1001:	**LATIN VULGATE "POCKET" BIBLE** Historiated initials perhaps by the Leber Atelier Illuminated manuscript on parchment Paris, France, possibly northeast France Circa 1230 GC.MS.000158	1004:	**NICHOLAS DE LYRA, *POSTILLAE LITTERALIS SUPER VETUS TESTAMENTUM* (COMMENTARY ON THE OLD TESTAMENT)** Copied by Egidius Alemanus Illuminated manuscript on parchment Italy, possibly Ferrara Circa 1451–1456 GC.MS.000335.1
1002:	**PSALTER FOR THE USE OF BRUSSELS** Illuminated manuscript on parchment Northern France, perhaps Paris Circa 1260 GC.MS.000323	1005:	**JOHANNES MARCHESINUS DE REGIO LEPIDI, *MAMMOTRECTUS SUPER BIBLIAM* (COMMENTARY ON THE BIBLE)** Decorated manuscript on paper and parchment Netherlands Circa 1460–1480 GC.MS.000164
1003:	**PSALTER** Illuminations possibly from the workshop of Johannes Grusch Illuminated manuscript on parchment Northern France, perhaps Paris Circa 1250–1270 GC.MS.000779		

manuscripts throughout Europe. The Paris Pocket Bibles, as manuscripts following this format came to be known, introduced many elements that still feature in modern Bibles. The text is written in two columns, with headings at the top of each page indicating which book of the Bible is being shown, and with the books arranged from Genesis to Revelation. The books are separated into chapters according to the system attributed to Stephen Langton (d. 1228), a professor at the University of Paris in the early 1200s.

Professional scribes often worked together with professional illuminators, who were responsible for the elaborate initials, page borders, and miniatures that decorate medieval manuscripts. Wealthy lay people commissioned highly embellished copies of personal devotional books like Psalters (Items 1002, 1003) and Books of Hours. Sometimes, these manuscripts can be linked to specific artists, such as the *Leber Atelier* (Item 1001), or to a collection of illuminators working in the same style, like the workshop of Johannes Grusch (Item 1003).

Occasionally, scribes would include endnotes called colophons in their writing, where they would sign their names, make comments, or include other bits of information. In the copy of Nicholas de Lyra's biblical commentary shown here (Item 1004), the main scribe—a man named Edigius Alemanus—signed and dated the manuscript each time he finished copying a large section of the text. According to the dates provided, Edigius spent more than five years copying this text and its accompanying volume before the work was finished by two other scribes.

The Gutenberg Press and the Advent of Printing

Johannes Gutenberg (ca. 1395-1468) was born into a family of well-to-do metal craftsmen in Mainz, Germany, where he was trained as a metalsmith from a young age. Around 1450, he began work on a project that would forever cement his place in the history books—the printing press.

Gutenberg's innovation was the use of moveable typeset to print. Previously, printers used a method called block printing, where an entire page was carved out of wood and inked to print multiple copies of the same page. Gutenberg's moveable typeset allowed a printer to manufacture an endless combination of pages easily and quickly, making it possible to produce many accurate copies of a single text, speeding up the production process, and making books infinitely more affordable.

The effects of Gutenberg's invention were enormous. Ideas spread across Europe—and the world—much more quickly than before, contributing to the flourishing of major intellectual movements such as the Renaissance, the Reformation, the Scientific Revolution, and the Enlightenment. Increasing the affordability of books meant that, for the first time, many texts—including the Bible—were available to more than just the wealthiest class of people. Gutenberg's invention forever changed the face of book production, and with it, the way that people were able to receive one of the most important books of all time, the Bible.

The Printing Revolution in the West   [Case 1100]

The first major work that Gutenberg printed with his movable typeset press was the Bible. Item 1101 is a so-called "noble fragment" of a Gutenberg Bible that contains the entire book of Romans. The text is in two columns of 42 lines, with a four-line decorated capital in red and blue added by hand, as were the heading and chapter numbers.

In contrast to Gutenberg's printed Bible, Item 1102 is a reproduction of the only complete block book in private hands in the United States. By design, block printing often featured elaborate illustrations to help convey the story to a largely illiterate population. The open page shows the Antichrist from the book of Revelation

Case 1100 – Item Diagnostics

1101:	LATIN BIBLE
	Noble Fragment containing the Epistle to the Romans
	Printed by Johann Gutenberg
	Ink on paper
	Mainz, Germany
	Circa 1454
	GC.INC.000142
1102:	*THE ANTICHRIST AND THE FIFTEEN SIGNS OF DOOMSDAY, BLOCK BOOK, FACSIMILE*
	Ink and pigment on paper
	Germany
	1470
	Reproduction of GC.INC.000153.1

1103:	LATIN BIBLE, FIRST EDITION WITH SCRIPTURAL CROSS-REFERENCES IN MARGINS
	Ink on paper
	Venice, Italy
	1483
	GC.INC.000146

(depicted with a dragon-like figure hovering over his head) interacting with a group of individuals, including a church official, a young aristocrat, and a rather caricatured elderly Jew. The original, owned by the Green Collection, is currently on display in Europe.

With the advent of printing came several new innovations in how the text of the Bible was presented that enhanced study. The final item in this case, a Latin Bible (Item 1103), was printed in Venice in 1483. It is the first edition of the Bible to contain biblical cross-references in the margins of the New Testament.

Other Early Printer Words   [Case 1200]

In addition to the Bible, other works began to be published soon after Gutenberg's invention. Anton Koberger's *Liber Cronicarum* (Item 1201)—an illustrated encyclopedia—was one of the most complicated and popular works printed in the late fifteenth century. It incorporated over 1,800 woodcut illustrations and chronicled human his-

Case 1200 – Item Diagnostics

1201:	NUREMBERG CHRONICLE, FIRST EDITION
	Printed by Anton Koberger
	Ink and pigment on paper
	Nuremberg, Germany
	1493
	GC.INC.000151
1202:	JOSEPHUS, *ANTIQUITY OF THE JEWS AND THE JEWISH WARS*, BOOK VII, FIRST EDITION
	Printed by Johannes Schussler
	Ink on paper
	Augsburg, Germany
	June 28–August 23, 1470
	GC.INC.000127

1203:	THOMAS AQUINAS, *SUMMA CONTRA GENTILES*
	Ink on paper
	Venice, Italy
	1476
	GC.INC.000123

tory from creation up through the time that the book was published. Item 1202 is Book VII of *Antiquity of the Jews and the Jewish Wars* by ancient Jewish historian Josephus (37-ca. 100), and Item 1203 is an edition of *Summa Contra Gentiles* by Thomas Aquinas (1225-1274), the most influential Christian theologian of the Middle Ages.

Religious Books for the Masses   [Case 1300]

The printing press made books of all kinds more accessible to a wider range of people. One of the most popular books was *The Imitation of Christ*, a devotional text by Thomas à Kempis. This copy of the first edition (Item 1301) is adorned by fine illustration. Indeed, many early printed books strived to look like earlier hand-copied manuscripts, meaning that layout, font, and illuminations were carefully thought out. Thomas à Kempis lived in Zwolle, Netherlands, where the Latin New Testament shown here (Item 1302) was produced. The Brothers of the Common Life, an early reform movement to which Thomas à Kempis belonged, copied this manuscript.

After the invention of the printing press, printers began to experiment with format and supplemental content when producing Bibles, anticipating a growing public market interested in Bible reading. One example of this (Item 1303) came from Italian printer Octavianus Scotus, who experimented with a small-format, octavo printing of the Bible for use by individuals and traveling preachers. Likewise, Johannes Froben of Basel, Switzerland, experimented with formats that made Bibles more affordable for the growing numbers of literate people. This so-called "Poor Man's Bible" (Item 1304) was published as a short octavo, making it less expensive, more portable, and easier to study than the larger-format Bibles.

The interesting hybrid book shown here (Item 1305) consists of a Psalter, printed in 1513 by Belgian printer Michael van Hoochstraten, and a manuscript portion containing a number of devotional and liturgical texts

Case 1300 – Item Diagnostics

1301:	THOMAS À KEMPIS, *THE IMITATION OF CHRIST*, FIRST EDITION	1304:	LATIN BIBLE, "POOR MAN'S BIBLE"
	Printed by Gunther Zainer		Printed by Johannes Froben
	Ink on paper		Ink on paper
	Augsburg, Germany		Basil, Switzerland
	Circa 1473		1491
	GC.INC.000138		GC.INC.000125
1302:	LATIN NEW TESTAMENT	1305:	DEVOTIONAL MISCELLANY WITH PRINTED PSALTER AND MANUSCRIPT DEVOTIONAL TEXTS
	Manuscript produced by		Printed by Michael van Hoochstraten; scribe unknown
	Brothers of the Common Life		Decorated hybrid book on paper
	Ink on parchment		Printed in Antwerp, Belgium; copied in Germany, possibly Bremen
	Zwolle, Netherlands		Circa 1513-1515
	1435		GC.MS.000116
	GC.MS.000281		
1303:	LATIN BIBLE		
	Printed by Octavianus Scotus		
	Ink on paper		
	Venice, Italy		
	1480		
	GC.INC.000144		

written in northern Germany between 1513 and 1515. The combination of printed and manuscript texts indicates a marked desire for works published in an affordable and in a portable format.

Early German Bibles   [Case 1400]

Among books printed in the so-called Incunable Period (books printed before 1500), one of the most influential is Item 1401, a ninth edition of the Bible in German printed by Anton Koberger. One of the most celebrated, innovative, and productive printers of this period, Koberger incorporated numerous woodcuts into the biblical text. Likewise, Item 1402—a compilation of New Testament readings translated into German from an original Latin text entitled the *Plenarium*—included a large number of woodcuts, leading to its common use for private devotion.

Case 1400 – Item Diagnostics

1401:	GERMAN BIBLE, NINTH EDITION	1402:	*EVANGELIEN UND EPISTELN*, GERMAN TRANSLATION OF THE *PLENARIUM*
	Printed by Anton Koberger		Printed by Johannes Schoensperger
	Ink and pigment on paper		Ink and pigment on paper
	Nuremberg, Germany		Augsburg, Germany
	1483		1495
	GC.INC.000136.2		GC.INC.000143

Questioning the Reliability of Printers   [Case 1500]

Though the printing press greatly improved the process of producing books, it was not an automatic cure from textual errors. Unfortunately, printers sometimes made mistakes when publishing their Bibles—mistakes that were not always caught until it was too late.

Case 1500 – Item Diagnostics

1501:	MATTHEWS BLACK LETTER "WIFE-BEATER" BIBLE
	Printed by Thomas Petyt
	Ink on paper
	London, England
	1551
	GC.BIB.000747
1502:	KING JAMES "HE" BIBLE, OLD TESTAMENT
	Printed by Robert Barker
	Ink on paper
	London, England
	1611
	GC.BIB.002770
1503:	KING JAMES "SHE" BIBLE
	Printed by Robert Barker
	Ink on paper
	London, England
	1613/1611
	GC.BIB.001206

This printing of the King James Great "He" Bible (Item 1602)—so named because it follows the Hebrew of the Masoretic Text (MT) and translates the pronoun in Ruth 3:15 in the masculine—notes on its title page, "The Holy Bible Conteyning the Old Testament and the New" but was nevertheless printed without the New Testament. The version next to it—the so-called Great "She" Bible (Item 1503), which uses the feminine pronoun for Ruth 3:15—corrects the error by including the New Testament. The different pronouns used in these two early King James Bibles show how variations in the transmission of the Bible can occur by deliberate decision, while the missing New Testament is an example of variation caused by mistake.

Some printers took deplorable liberties with the texts they were meant to be reproducing faithfully. For instance, the so-called "Wife-Beater" Bible (Item 1501) received its name due to a marginal note for

1 Peter 3:7, added by the printer Edmund Becke. It states, "And if she be not obediente and healpful unto hym, endevoureth to beate the fere of God into her heade, that thereby she may be compelled to learne her dutye and do it."

Typos, Misprints, and Errors   [Case 1600]

Other examples of mistakes in Bible printing include the so-called "Child Killer" Bible (Item 1601) where Mark 7:27 reads, "let the children first be killed" instead of "filled." In the so-called "Judas" Bible (Items 1602, 1603), the text of Matthew 26:36 reads, "Then cometh Judas with them" instead of "Jesus with them." At some point, an owner of Item 1603 roughly corrected the error by hand.

Case 1600 – Item Diagnostics

1601:	THE "CHILD KILLER" BIBLE	1603:	THE "JUDAS" BIBLE, CORRECTED
	Printed by Thomas Bensley		Printed by Robert Barker
	Ink on paper		Ink on paper
	Oxford, England		London, England
	1795		1613/1611
	GC.BIB.000228.2		GC.BIB.000201
1602:	THE "JUDAS" BIBLE		
	Printed by Robert Barker		
	Ink on paper		
	London, England		
	1613/1611		
	GC.BIB.001059		

When a Typo Turns the Bible "Wicked"   [Case 1700]

The King James "Wicked" Bible (Item 1701) features one of the most notorious typographical errors in Bible printing history: one of the Ten Commandments omits the very important command "not." Thus, Exodus 20:14 reads, "Thou shalt commit adultery" instead of "Thou shalt not." Only 1000 of these misprints were made, and

Case 1700 – Item Diagnostics

1701:	KING JAMES "WICKED" BIBLE	1703:	KING JAMES "UNRIGHTEOUS" BIBLE
	Printed by Robert Barker		Printed by John Field
	Ink on paper		Ink on paper
	London, England		London, England
	1631		1653
	GC.BIB.002902		GC.BIB.001691
1702:	KING JAMES "WICKED" BIBLE, CORRECTED WITH NEW LEAF		
	Printed by Robert Barker		
	Ink on paper		
	London, England		
	1631		
	GC.BIB.000197		

the printers were fined £300 for the offense—at that time, a sizeable amount. Item 1702 represents a corrected version of the "Wicked" Bible, where the original page was cut out and replaced with a new, error-free leaf.

The "Unrighteous" Bible (Item 1703), printed in 1653, contains several misprints. For instance, 1 Corinthians 6:9 says, "Know ye not that the unrighteous shall inherit the kingdom of God" instead of "shall not inherit the kingdom of God." Here, Romans 6:13 reads, "Neither yield ye your members as instruments of righteousness unto sin." It should have said "as instruments of unrighteousness unto sin." In a final example, Matthew 6:24 reads "Ye cannot serve and mammon" instead of "serve God and Mammon."

The Tent of Discovery and the Cairo Genizah

A major part of the story of any text's transmission is not only how it originally passed from one person to the next, but also how it has survived to the present day. Since the nineteenth century, several discoveries have been made which provide earlier witnesses to the texts of the Bible than existed previously. Unlike a manuscript such as the Great Isaiah Scroll, which survived for two thousand years because it was stored in a jar in a cave, many of the items that you encounter in the Tent of Discovery were not intentionally preserved. In fact, they survived precisely because people discarded or reused these biblical manuscripts for other purposes. Papyrus was recycled to make a stiffening material (cartonnage), ink was washed or scraped off the parchment to write newer manuscripts, and worn-out copies were dumped in trash heaps. Alongside these textual discoveries, you can explore some of the tools that help scholars to study and date biblical texts, tools ranging from interdisciplinary perspectives in archaeology to cutting-edge imaging technologies.

Beyond the tent lies the Ben Ezra Synagogue. Located in Cairo, Egypt, this synagogue preserved one of the most important collections of medieval Jewish religious texts ever found. They had accumulated through the practice of retiring worn-out copies of texts containing the divine name—which included biblical manuscripts—to a special storage area called a *genizah*, in preparation for an honored burial. As you enter, you will see a pair of synagogue officials depositing texts in the *genizah*, and three cases displaying fragments from it.

Unearthing Texts in Context   [Case 1800]
The items in this case offer a small sampling of archaeology's multifaceted contributions to understanding both the transmission of biblical texts and their content.

The two fragmentary manuscripts both come from the rubbish heaps of Oxyrhynchus [pronounced *äk-si-ˈriŋ-kəs*]. In Greco-Roman times, Oxyrhynchus was a prosperous regional capital in southern Egypt. For centuries, private citizens and government officials dumped their old documents and worn-out manuscripts in trash heaps outside this city. Over time, the mounds were covered with sand, and the texts quietly survived in a climate that does not experience rain or flooding. In the late 1800s, two students from Oxford, Bernard Grenfell and Arthur Hunt, began a series of excavations that unearthed thousands of texts, including numerous copies of biblical texts. Most were on papyri (Item 1809) but some were on parchment (Item 1808). These discoveries represent over 30% of known New Testament papyri today. That these texts were found together with a wealth of material about everyday life—land contracts, personal letters, marriage and divorce documents, household accounts, and more—helps us to study these biblical manuscripts in connection with the people who used them.

Other artifacts in this case exemplify how material culture other than manuscripts also sheds light on the diverse communities and individuals who transmitted the Bible. For example, incantation, or magic, bowls were commonly used in the Ancient Near East to ward off evil. Placed under thresholds or in corners of a room, some provide fascinating evidence for the use of biblical passages. The bowl shown here (Item 1807) has an inscription that quotes Isaiah 22:16-19 followed by Isaiah 22:8.

Archaeological discoveries can also illuminate specific biblical references. The small bronze *prutah* (Item 1804), one of the smallest amounts in the currency of Roman Judea, was worth two *lepta*, the amount of the widow's offering in Mark 12:41-44. While these were of very little monetary worth in the first century, their historical value today is quite high, since these small coins provide some of the earliest surviving inscriptions in both Hebrew and paleo-Hebrew scripts. In addition, their iconography provides a window into the ideology of people living in Roman Palestine.

Any time coins are found within a clear archaeological context (such as the floor of an excavated building or the wall of a house), they may help date associated materials with greater accuracy. Similarly, the oil lamps displayed here (Items 1801, 1802, 1803), which have had the same function for over a thousand years, show subtle differences in form and manufacture that help archaeologists identify their original historical context.

Case 1800 – Item Diagnostics

1801:	OIL LAMP Terracotta, partly wheel-thrown and partly handmade Eastern Mediterranean Late Bronze Age, circa 15th–12th century BC GC.CER.000362	1806:	BYZANTINE "JESUS" COIN Bronze Byzantium 10th century AD GC.NUM.000848
1802:	OIL LAMPS Terracotta, mold-made Eastern Mediterranean Hellenistic period, 4th–1st century BC GC.CER.000259, GC.CER.000260	1807:	INCANTATION BOWL WITH TEXT FROM ISAIAH 22 Ink on ceramic base Sassanian Asoristan/Abbasid Iraq Circa 4th century AD GC.MBL.000165
1803:	OIL LAMP Terracotta, mold-made Eastern Mediterranean Herodian period, 1st century BC–1st century AD GC.CER.000261	1808:	P. OXY. 1353 1 PETER 5 IN GREEK Ink on parchment Oxyrhynchus, Egypt 4th century AD GC.MS.000284
1804:	PRUTAH COINS, A.K.A. "WIDOW'S MITES" Bronze Roman Judaea 1st century BC GC.NUM.000356, GC.NUM.000357, GC.NUM.000358	1809:	P. OXY. 1779 PSALM 1:4-6 IN GREEK Ink on papyrus Oxyrhynchus, Egypt 4th century AD GC.PAP.000445
1805:	SOLIDUS COINS DEPICTING VARIOUS BYZANTINE EMPERORS Gold Byzantium 7th century AD GC.NUM.000682, GC.NUM.000685, GC.NUM.000686, GC.NUM.000687, GC.NUM.000688, GC.NUM.000689, GC.NUM.000690		

Recovering Recycled Manuscripts [Case 1900]

The items in this case illustrate two different recycling procedures from ancient times. Each unintentionally preserved portions of discarded biblical manuscripts, and today researchers can examine these procedures to regain access to those biblical texts.

As a writing material made from plant fibers, old used papyrus was sometimes converted into a stiffening material known as cartonnage, through a process similar to the making of paper mache. People used cartonnage to make elaborate objects, such as painted mummy masks (Item 1901), and simpler items, such as sandal bottoms and the flat round disks shown here (Item 1902). Since the late 1800s, when British archaeologist Flinders Petrie first discovered that papyrus fragments could be recovered from mummy cases, scraps of ancient writing ranging from documents concerning everyday life to literature by authors such as Homer and Plato to biblical texts have been found in cartonnage. The fragments of 1 Samuel in Greek shown here (Item 1903) were recovered from flat disks similar to the ones in this case.

Since extracting texts often requires dismantling the object that contains them, the existence of cartonnage raises a difficult choice: Should we regain one historical witness (the writing) or retain the other (the object)? Both are important in their own ways. As a result, museums and other institutions committed to preserving cultural heritage are now exploring non-invasive techniques to "read through" layers of papyrus. Two options attempted in recent years are CT scanning (using medical equipment) and terahertz time-domain spectroscopy. Although both techniques are only in the early stages of experimentation, there is hope that such technology might develop further to facilitate both the preservation of historical objects and access to the texts they conceal.

The Codex Climaci Rescriptus (CCR) is a palimpsest. A palimpsest is new document written over an erased text underneath. The brown ink still visible on this leaf (Item 1904) shows how erasure was not always complete, and the result is a page with one layer of text superimposed on another. The CCR reused parchment from not just one older manuscript but at least ten different codices in two different languages. To see sample differences, compare the leaf in this case with the one shown on the iPad (in the corner of the tent), which reused parchment from a copy of the Gospels written in Christian Palestinian Aramaic. The black text on top is written in the same handwriting, but the brownish texts underneath are not. By applying multi-spectral imaging (MSI)—a technique that photographs each page under different wavelengths of light—to palimpsests, we are improving researchers' access to the older, underlying texts in manuscripts like the CCR.

Case 1900 – Item Diagnostics

1901:	POLYCHROME AND GILT CARTONNAGE MUMMY MASK Painted gesso over linen and papyrus Egypt Circa 1st century BC to 1st century AD GC.MMY.000152
1902:	CARTONNAGE DISKS Ink and papyrus Egypt Possibly 4th–5th century AD GC.PAP.000398
1903:	1 SAMUEL 4-5 IN GREEK Ink on papyrus Egypt Late 4th–5th century AD GC.PAP.000416
1904:	LEAF FROM THE CODEX CLIMACI RESCRIPTUS, BIBLICAL LECTIONARY IN CHRISTIAN PALESTINIAN ARAMAIC REUSED FOR "THE LADDER OF DIVINE ASCENT" IN SYRIAC Ink on parchment Sinai, Egypt Circa 6th century AD and 9th century AD GC.MS.000149.78

Reflectance Transformation Imaging (Interactive Display)

This *bulla* (clay stamped with a seal impression) contains an inscription, which is difficult to read under normal light conditions. If you looked at this object with a handheld light source, moving the light back and forth, you might be able to see more of the inscription than you can under flat light (light providing no shadows). However, with the technology on display here—Reflectance Transformation Imaging (RTI)—much, much more can be seen. The photographs of the *bulla* included in this display are produced using three different lighting conditions:

1. Visible light—standard photograph with no technical enhancement
2. Diffuse gain—boosted light contrast of the visible surface, making the degree of depth and other variables on the surface texture of the object more evident
3. Specular reflection—under varying light conditions, with the light coming from different directions, the surface information of the object can be brought into greater or lesser visibility, by aiming the light from whichever direction is brightest, illuminating the object's surface by producing an artificial or "specular" enhancement

These imaging applications help us gain a considerable amount of information about an object. For instance, when the *bulla* is imaged with diffuse light gain, fingerprints which are not immediately evident under visible light become starkly evident.

When used on manuscripts, RTI enhancement (also known as "polynomial texture mapping") can yield information about the "scribal hand" or handwriting characteristics present. When the edges of strokes on letters are made more discernable by way of light reflection, we can make more sophisticated and technical comparisons of scribes' individual strokes between manuscripts, enhancing our ability to link individual manuscripts to specific scribes. This is understandably a very exciting realization for the world of Dead Sea Scrolls studies where the majority of the nearly 1,000 manuscripts discovered in one area date within 100 years of each other. It is quite possible that with the application of these new imaging techniques and time, we will be able to begin grouping surviving manuscripts according to the specific scribal hands that produced them.

Thanks to imaging advancements pioneered jointly by Hewlett Packard labs and the West Semitic Research Project, Museum of the Bible is able to apply some of the most sophisticated techniques in photography to its collections.

Recovering a Millennium's Worth of Manuscripts (Cairo Genizah Diorama)

After the Dead Sea Scrolls, perhaps the most important discovery of Jewish manuscripts is the "Cairo Genizah," a collection of some 300,000 Jewish manuscript fragments that roughly date between AD 870 and AD 1880. These manuscripts were found in the *genizah* of the Ben Ezra Synagogue located in Fustat, or Old Cairo, Egypt.

As was the case with some of the manuscripts on display in the previous room, these manuscripts were never intended to survive into the present day. The Jewish code of laws, known as the Talmud, dictates that when Jewish manuscripts containing the name of God (particularly those of a biblical nature) are irreparably damaged or in a state of disuse, they are not to be discarded, but rather retired to a storeroom, or *genizah*, until a ceremonial burial can be prepared. Today, most synagogues have some such storeroom where texts containing the sacred name are collected before burial. What makes the *genizah* at Ben Ezra Synagogue unique is that, for nearly a thousand years, none of the manuscripts were removed and buried.

Since Jews treat their religious texts with such great respect in this way, ancient and medieval Jewish manuscripts are much scarcer than their Christian counterparts are. Therefore, the discoveries made in the Ben Ezra

Synagogue have huge implications for scholars who study the history of Judaism and the textual transmission of the Hebrew Bible.

An Abundant Storeroom and a Window into Medieval Judaism   [Case 2000]

The wider academic community has only know the contents of the Cairo Genizah, and their importance, during last three centuries. In the mid-eighteenth century, a European traveler named Simon van Gelderen mentioned the existence of such a room in his writings, but offered no further commentary. Roughly a century later, the repository was "rediscovered" by an Eastern European scholar named Jacob Saphir, who was the first to remark on the potential significance of the collection's contents. It was not until 1896, however, when two sisters traveling from England—Agnes S. Lewis and Margaret D. Gibson—acquired a sample of manuscripts for identification and study, sharing them with scholar Solomon Schechter at Cambridge University, that the significance of the collection was fully realized.

The contents of the Cairo Genizah are unique not only for the chronological breadth demonstrated, but also for the variety of subjects represented. The *genizah* contained numerous religious texts, such as Torahs, prayer books for daily use (Items 2004, 2005, 2007), and special prayers for fasts (Item 2001) and holidays, like Pass-

Case 2000 – Item Diagnostics

2001:	PRAYERS FOR DAYS OF FASTING FROM KARAITE PRAYER BOOK **Fragment discovered in the Cairo Genizah** Ink on Paper Egypt 12th century AD GC.PPR.010103	2005:	CONFESSION OF SINS FROM A KARAITE PRAYER BOOK **Fragment discovered in the Cairo Genizah** Ink on Paper Egypt Circa AD 1280–1330 GC.PPR.010093
2002:	PRAYERS FOR PASSOVER MORNING FROM KARAITE PRAYER BOOK, WITH INSTRUCTIONS IN ARABIC **Fragment discovered in the Cairo Genizah** Ink on Paper Egypt 14th century AD GC.PPR.010087.1-.3	2006:	PENITENTIAL PRAYERS (ORDER OF *SELICHOT*) FOR YOM KIPPUR MORNING FROM A KARAITE PRAYER BOOK **Fragment discovered in the Cairo Genizah** Ink on Paper Egypt Circa AD 1300 GC.PPR.010092
2003:	PRAYERS FOR THE FEAST OF UNLEAVENED BREAD FROM KARAITE PRAYER BOOK **Fragment discovered in the Cairo Genizah** Ink on Paper Egypt 13th century AD GC.PPR.010090.1-.2	2007:	SUPPLICATIONS FROM A KARAITE PRAYER BOOK **Fragment discovered in the Cairo Genizah** Ink on Paper Egypt Circa AD 1330 GC.PPR.010134.1-.2
2004:	PORTION OF A KARAITE PRAYER BOOK **Fragment discovered in the Cairo Genizah** Ink on Paper Egypt 13th century AD GC.PPR.010114		

over (Items 2002, 2003) and Yom Kippur (Item 2006). It also contained a number of secular documents, from marriage contracts and medical books to shopping lists and personal letters. As a result, it is an unparalleled source for understanding the everyday lives of medieval Jews.

Karaite Judaism and Biblical Literalism   [Case 2100]

The Jews of the Ben Ezra Synagogue in Old Cairo were Rabbanite Jews, which means that they accepted the authority of rabbinical interpretation of the Torah and the Talmud. The contents of the Cairo Genizah, however, also include religious manuscripts from other movements in Judaism, such as the Karaite sect. While Rabbanite Jews believe that the Talmud represents an oral tradition of law handed down by God in addition to the laws written in the Torah, the Karaites, which means "People of the Scripture" or "Scripturalists," hold to a strict interpretation of the literal words contained in the Bible. Accordingly, they reject the idea of an "oral Torah."

These fragments shown here from Karaite prayer books, found among the Cairo Genizah hoard, reflect the sect's commitment to strict use and interpretation of the Bible. Unlike the Rabbanite Jews, who incorporated a number of rabbinic prayers into their liturgy, Karaites typically restricted their prayer services to the Psalms and other passages from the Bible.

The inclusion of Karaite material in a Rabbanite *genizah* suggests that we should be cautious about overemphasizing the divide between the two communities.

Studying the Cairo Genizah at Cambridge [Case 2200]

Perhaps no name is more closely associated with the Cairo Genizah than that of Solomon Schechter (1847-1915). Born at a time when Eastern Europe was a major hub of Jewish learning, this Moldavian rabbi quickly rose in academic ranks to a position of great prestige at the University of Cambridge. By the age of 43, he had joined the faculty of theology there, teaching the Talmud and Rabbinical Studies.

At the age of 49, he was told of a significant corpus of ancient biblical manuscripts from the *genizah* of the Ben Ezra Synagogue in Cairo, Egypt. Upon securing the capital to support his expedition, Schechter traveled to Cairo, on behalf of the university, where he

Case 2100 – Item Diagnostics

2101:	THE *KEDUSHAH* SECTION OF PRAYERS FROM A KARAITE PRAYER BOOK **Fragment discovered in the Cairo Genizah** Ink on Paper Egypt 14th century AD GC.PPR.010073.1-.3
2102:	EVENING PRAYERS FOR THE DAY OF BLOWING THE SHOFAR FROM A KARAITE PRAYER BOOK **Fragment discovered in the Cairo Genizah** Ink on Paper Egypt 14th century AD GC.PPR.010096.1-.2
2103:	PRAYERS FOR YOM KIPPUR FROM A KARAITE PRAYER BOOK **Fragment discovered in the Cairo Genizah** Ink on Paper Egypt 14th century AD GC.PPR.010129
2104:	PRAYERS FOR THE FASTS OF THE SEVENTH AND TENTH DAYS OF *AV* FROM A KARAITE PRAYER BOOK **Fragment discovered in the Cairo Genizah** Ink on Paper Egypt 14th–15th century AD GC.PPR.010133
2105:	THE "GREAT HALLEL" (PSALM 136) FROM A KARAITE PRAYER BOOK, PRAYED ON THE SABBATH BEFORE PASSOVER **Fragment discovered in the Cairo Genizah** Ink on Paper Egypt Circa AD 1530 GC.PPR.010106

worked with local rabbinical leaders and was given permission to remove what he liked. He purchased some 193,000 manuscripts, famously explaining later, "I liked it all." This significant acquisition now forms part of the Taylor-Schechter Collection at the Cambridge University Library. The picture behind this case shows Schechter in 1898, working in the room at the library where the manuscripts were stored.

Schechter later became a prominent figure in the United States, serving as both founder and President of the United Synagogue of America and President of the Jewish Theological Seminary in New York.

Case 2200 – Item Diagnostics

2201:	THE *KEDUSHAH* SECTION OF PRAYERS FROM A KARAITE PRAYER BOOK **Fragment discovered in the Cairo Genizah** Ink on Paper Egypt 13th century AD GC.PPR.010111	2205:	PRAYER FOR THE SEVENTH DAY OF *AV* FROM A KARAITE PRAYER BOOK **Fragment discovered in the Cairo Genizah** Ink on Paper Egypt 14th century AD GC.PPR.010084.1-.3
2202:	PORTION OF A KARAITE PRAYER BOOK **Fragment discovered in the Cairo Genizah** Ink on Paper Egypt 13th century AD GC.PPR.010113	2206:	PORTION OF A KARAITE PRAYER BOOK, WITH INSTRUCTIONS IN ARABIC **Fragment discovered in the Cairo Genizah** Ink on Paper Egypt 14th century AD GC.PPR.010128
2203:	PORTION OF A KARAITE PRAYER BOOK **Fragment discovered in the Cairo Genizah** Ink on Paper Egypt 13th century AD GC.PPR.010136	2207:	PORTION OF A KARAITE PRAYER BOOK FOR HOLIDAYS **Fragment discovered in the Cairo Genizah** Ink on Paper Egypt 14th century AD GC.PPR.010132
2204:	PRAYER FOR THE TORAH SECTION *HA'AZINU* FROM A KARAITE PRAYER BOOK **Fragment discovered in the Cairo Genizah** Ink on Paper Egypt 13th–14th century AD GC.PPR.010094.1-.2		

The Lunar Bible: The First Book on the Moon

Throughout history, a wide variety of methods and technologies has been used to transport the Bible around the world. The story of biblical transmission, however, extends beyond the Earth to the surface of the moon itself.

In 1969, the Apollo 11 mission carried Neil Armstrong and Edwin "Buzz" Aldrin to the surface of the moon, opening up a new avenue for human exploration, and allowing the Bible to travel farther than it ever had before.

Although the words of the Bible had travelled into space on several previous missions, the first Bibles did not physically reach the moon until 1971. On February 5, 1971, Apollo 14 Astronaut Edgar Mitchell carried the first copies of the Bible to the lunar surface. Due to weight restrictions for astronauts' personal items, the only Bibles that could make the 384,400-kilometer journey to the moon were copies printed using microform technology. This allowed all 1,245 pages and 773,746 words of the King James Bible to be condensed onto a piece of film 4-centimeter square.

This gallery contains several artifacts that represent key moments in the history of the written word: cuneiform tablets, papyrus scrolls, manuscript codices on parchment, and printed books.

Finally, you will see one of the microfiche Bibles that made the 238,900-mile journey to the moon.

Cuneiform Tablets: The First System of Writing   [Case 2300]

This cuneiform tablet represents the earliest form of writing in human history. Cuneiform was developed over 5,000 years ago in southern Iraq as temple overseers sought better ways to manage their inventories and workers.

Case 2300 – Item Diagnostics

2301:	UR III ROYAL MESSENGER TABLET
	Clay
	Southern Iraq
	Circa 2050 BC
	GC.CUN.000218

Scribes wrote by taking a pointed reed and making impressions in wet clay. Most documents were written to record administrative, business, or legal transactions. Item 2301 lists beer and bread allotments for royal messengers.

Though cuneiform tablets do not contain biblical texts, cuneiform sources do provide scholars with information about the history and culture of the Ancient Near Eastern societies mentioned in the Hebrew Bible.

Papyrus Scrolls: A New Step in the Portability of Writing   [Case 2400]

Shortly after cuneiform was first used in Mesopotamia, Egyptians began writing on a very different material and in a different format: the papyrus scroll. Papyrus is a material made from the fibers of a reed-like plant grown in Egypt. For over three thousand years of Egyptian history and extending into Greco-Roman times, texts were written on papyrus scrolls, like Item 2401.

Case 2400 – Item Diagnostics

2401:	PAPYRUS SCROLL
	Papyrus and string
	Likely Egypt
	Use flourished circa 3000 BC–AD 200
	GC.PAP.000130

This Egyptian scroll is still tied with a hemp string, which was sometimes used with a seal from the person sending the letter or document.

Manuscript Codices on Parchment: The Scroll becomes a Book   [Case 2500]

About the fourth century AD, books began to surpass scrolls as the primary way to record texts. The book, or codex, revolutionized the way texts were read, because they allowed a reader to flip back and forth and compare different portions of the text more easily than in a scroll. Although the codex was not invented by Christians, its widespread use was closely intertwined with the spread of Christianity. In the early centuries of the codex, papyrus was used for pages, but eventually papyrus gave way to parchment, a writing surface made from the skin animals, like sheep or cattle. Like the tablets and scrolls that preceded them, medieval codices were manuscripts, meaning they were written by hand.

The manuscript in this case (Item 2501) contains a biblical commentary by Petrus Riga. The commentary, *Aurora*, is also known as "the versified Bible" because it consists largely of poetic paraphrases of the Bible.

Case 2500 – Item Diagnostics

2501:	PETRUS RIGA, *AURORA* (BIBLICAL COMMENTARY)
	Decorated manuscript on parchment
	Italy
	Circa AD 1230
	GC.MS.000370

Printing, Translation, and Authorization: The King James Bible   [Case 2600]

About AD 1450, Johannes Gutenberg invented the printing press, and with it, books became more accessible than ever before. Less than a century later, the Protestant Reformation created a renewed and fervent interest in Bible translation. These two events led to the widespread production of vernacular Bibles that exemplifies biblical transmission in the Modern Era.

Case 2600 – Item Diagnostics

2601:	KING JAMES BIBLE, SECOND QUARTO EDITION
	Printed by Robert Barker
	Ink on paper
	London, England
	1613
	GC.BIB.003692

The King James Bible—an English translation authorized by King James I of England—was first printed in 1611. The following year, the first copies of the King James Bible were printed in quarto-size (Item 2601), making it more affordable and more manageable for personal use. To this day, the King James Bible remains the most popular English translation of the Bible.

Microform and Space Travel: Putting the First Bible on the Moon   [Case 2700]

On February 5, 1971, the Bible became the first book to land on another celestial body.

The desire to take a copy of the Bible to the moon was first expressed by Edward White II, Senior Pilot on Apollo 1. When a tragic cabin fire killed him and his fellow crewmembers less than a month before their scheduled launch date, NASA chaplain John Stout formed the Apollo Prayer League, an organization that would work to see that White's dream was fulfilled.

One of the first difficulties faced by the Apollo Prayer League was the weight restrictions NASA placed on astronauts' personal items. The answer was microform, a technology that involves creating a micro-reproduction of an image—usually one-twenty-fifth of the original size—on small flat sheets (microfiche) or rolls (microfilm) of film. The Apollo Prayer League attempted to have a copy of the Bible taken to the moon aboard both Apollo 12 and Apollo 13, but for different reasons both attempts were unsuccessful. The group was finally successful with the Apollo 14 mission, when Lunar Module

Case 2700 – Item Diagnostics

2701:	**COMPLETE LUNAR BIBLE**
	Travelled to the Moon during the Apollo 14 mission
	Microfilm in gold frame
	United States
	February 5, 1971
	GC.BIB.003832

Pilot Edgar D. Mitchell carried 100 copies of the King James Bible on microfiche to the surface of the moon inside his "Personal Preference Kit Bag."

This case contains one of only twelve complete Lunar Bibles (Item 2701), dual-certified by Edgar Mitchell and Reverend John Stout of the Apollo Prayer League. After returning to earth, most of the "Lunar Bibles" were segmented into fifty- and two-page fragments and distributed to various political figures by the Apollo Prayer League, who had sponsored the Bible's trip to the moon.

The Bible in the Digital Age

Today, there is not a single aspect of life that is not touched by technology. Social media connects people all around the world, and tablets and smartphones make a world of information so accessible that everything there is to know seems to be no more than a tap of the finger away.

Digital technology is revolutionizing the world of Bible transmission. More than 2,000 smartphone apps allow users to download the Bible free. One of the more popular applications, the YouVersion Bible App™, has already been downloaded on more than 170 million devices. Users can access the Bible in many languages, sometimes with options for side-by-side comparisons of different translations. Meanwhile, social media platforms like Facebook, Twitter, and Instagram are making individual interactions with the Bible more visible than ever before. It is now possible to see who is talking about the Bible in real time all over the world.

In more remote parts of the world, technology plays a different role in Bible transmission. Teams working on bringing the Bible to these communities use special software programs to facilitate translation, and satellite internet networks speed up their work.

The Bible—There's an App for That (Interactive Display)

Smart devices have changed the way people access information. We expect to be able to check email, look up any fact, or post a status with just the tap of a finger. It seems like there is an app for everything.

Searching for "Bible" on the app store returns more than 2,000 results. The most popular version—with more than 170 million downloads—is the YouVersion Bible App™. The free app, created by Oklahoma pastor Bobby Gruenewald and his team at LifeChurch.tv, launched in 2008. In the first weekend, more than 83,000 people downloaded it.

The app contains more than 1,000 versions of the Bible in over 700 languages. Users can switch between versions to compare translations, use bookmarks or highlighting features to personalize their interaction with the Bible, and share verses directly to social media. The app also includes hundreds of reading plans that recommend selections of daily reading from the Bible and other resources.

This display allows you to check out how people around the world are interacting with the Bible App™. You can also explore the app for yourself, using the interactive stations provided.

Providing Remote Access in Remote Locations   [Case 2800]

Bible transmission is an ongoing process. The Bible is readily available on every continent and in every major language, but there are still many places around the world where people cannot access the Bible in their own language. Today, translation and linguistic development projects are actively taking place in 131 countries for more than 2,300 languages. New technologies are improving the speed and accuracy with which these projects are completed.

One of the biggest challenges that the modern translation teams working on these projects face is limited communication. Large distances—sometimes days—separate team members from places with internet access. This greatly impedes the translation process, particularly when translators are attempting to have their work checked by others. Recently, however, the use of Broadband Global Area Network (BGAN) terminals help address this problem. BGAN terminals (Item 2801) provide users with worldwide satellite internet coverage, and can be paired with alternative power sources, like solar panels, to improve the speed with which translators are able to relay information to their team members—wherever they are.

Case 2800 – Item Diagnostics

2801:	BROADBAND GLOBAL AREA NETWORK (BGAN) SATELLITE TERMINAL AND POWER SOURCE
	Wideye Sabre 1 Model
	Mixed materials
	21st century
	Loan courtesy of Wycliffe Bible Translators

Many software programs and technological initiatives are improving the process of Bible transmission in the digital age. The translation software Paratext™ was developed by the United Bible Societies and SIL International, and is designed specifically to facilitate Bible translation. It understands how the Bible is structured and allows easy comparison with the biblical text in its original languages. Adapt It™ is another commonly used program that takes linguistic principles from languages similar to the one being used for a new translation and applies those to that target language, resulting in a projected translation with 70% accuracy. SIL International also runs the Non-Roman Script Initiative, which is improving the way computers process alphabets that work differently from the Latin alphabet used by most Western languages.

To learn more about how these technological initiatives are improving the process of bringing the Bible to the most remote parts of the globe, watch the video in the corner of this area.

Using Augmented Reality to Bring the Bible to Life (Interactive Displays)

Every day, new technologies are being developed that have the potential to radically affect the way we access information and interact with the world around us—including the Bible.

One such technology is Augmented Reality (AR). Augmented Reality is the process of adding a digital layer on top of a view of the real world (like a page in a book). Using a smart device and an AR reader, you are able to unlock and view digital content—video, 3D objects, images, and so on—that seems to be "hidden" in the world around you. Due to the ever-growing dependence on digital devices and the need for more natural ways of accessing digital content in everyday life, many top tech companies, from Apple to Google, are pouring their resources into AR development and implementation. It is likely that we will continue to see more of this technology in the future.

AR technology has enormous potential for enriching the way that people engage with different subjects, including the Bible. The Bible has a vast amount of commentary, visuals, and other background information that can greatly improve our understanding of and interaction with the text. AR provides one way of putting all of that information directly at a person's fingertips. Point an AR reader at a map, for example, and the map becomes three-dimensional, allowing you to zoom in or out, explore the surrounding area, and learn more about different features highlighted on the map itself. Likewise, images on a page can become "real" 3D objects and video tours allow you to step into the picture and look around.

Use the interactive stations in the gallery to check out Museum of the Bible's implementation of Augmented Reality for yourself.

Interactive Station 1—Travels of Abraham (Map)
"The Lord had said to Abram, 'Go from your country, your people and your father's household to the land I will show you.'" Genesis 12:1 (NIV)

Interactive Station 2—Seven Species of Israel (Quiz)
"A land of wheat and barley, of vines and fig trees and pomegranates, a land of olive trees and honey." Deuteronomy 8:8 (ESV)

Interactive Station 3—Great Ziggurat of Ur (Video)
Ur is the best known of the Sumerian cities. Step into the great Ziggurat of Ur in southern Iraq.

Movement 2—Controversy

The Bible is a radical text with a provocative history. From its earliest beginnings to the present, its words have been surrounded by controversy, and in every century people have wrestled with what exactly the Bible is, what it means, and how it ought to be used.

In the first few centuries AD, both Jews and Christians engaged in debates to determine which books should be included in their Bibles. This resulted in lists that differ—sometimes greatly—between various Jewish and Christian traditions. Disagreements over how to interpret the Bible correctly have led to religious division and even political upheaval. Some people have tried to stamp the Bible out of existence, while others have sacrificed and died for its preservation. And many people have used it to justify and defend their actions, for example, in situations like slavery, apartheid, and the Holocaust.

This section takes a closer look at some of the more divisive moments in the Bible's history.

The Biblical Canon: A Collection of Collections

The Bible is a collection of writings composed over many centuries. Today these writings are often printed together as a single book. Prior to the 300s AD, however, no one-volume Bibles existed, and such Bibles remained very rare until the 1200s.

For many centuries, most readers encountered the Bible as a library of multiple scrolls or volumes. A biblical "canon" is the full set of writings that a religious community accepts as belonging in this library, because it regards them as being uniquely authoritative. Exactly which titles are included? How are they organized? Various Jewish and Christian traditions have answered these questions similarly on some points and differently on others. For example, every biblical canon begins with the same five books and treats them as a distinct group, known as the "Torah" ("Law" or "Teaching") or "Pentateuch." By comparison, not every biblical canon includes the same number, selection, or sequence of books under the heading of "Prophets."

Jewish and Christian communities collected the books of the Bible in multiple stages. Smaller groupings such as the Torah or the Gospels were formed before the canon as a whole had fully developed. Deliberate attention to biblical canon arose after major events, such as the destruction of the Jerusalem Temple in AD 70 and Constantine's conversion to Christianity in AD 312. Such events triggered various debates and controversies, which motivated people to write out canon lists. Leaders reviewed which books their communities had already accepted as uniquely authoritative, and discussed why they belonged in the canon.

Canon and Controversy   [Case 3000]

All Christian Bibles today contain two major collections: the "Old Testament" and the "New Testament." The Protestant Old Testament contains the same books as the Jewish Bible, but in a different order (compare Item 3002 with Item 3001). The Old Testament of Roman Catholic, Eastern Orthodox, and other Christian traditions includes more books (compare Items 3004, 3005 with 3001, 3002). Some Protestant Bibles list these books under the heading "Apocrypha," as traditional but not canonical (Item 3003). How did these similarities and differences arise?

In the first and second centuries AD, the debates that most drastically influenced biblical canon concerned one question: Did the God of Israel—the God depicted in the sacred writings of the Jewish people—send Jesus of Nazareth as the anticipated Messiah?

Disagreement began within Judaism. Some Jews believed that Jesus fulfilled the expectations found in their sacred writings (Genesis, Joshua, Isaiah, Psalms, etc.). They studied those texts to help them understand Jesus' life and teachings. They also composed additional writings to explain connections between Jesus and the God of Israel. Other Jews believed that the message of Jesus' early followers was incompatible with their ancestral texts. They regarded the newer writings as blasphemous, and eventually declared that they should be rejected.

After the Temple was destroyed in AD 70, Christianity gradually became a separate religion with new challenges. Some who accepted the new writings began questioning the old ones. Around AD 144, an influential Christian teacher named Marcion argued that the Jewish scriptures (Genesis, Joshua, Psalms, etc.) depicted an inferior "god" of wrath, different from Jesus' God of love, and should thus be rejected. Since Jesus' early followers linked his life to these older books, Marcion also rejected many of their writings, including the Gospels of Matthew and John. Marcion's "biblical canon" approved only Luke's Gospel plus ten of Paul's letters, all shortened to fit Marcion's views.

Case 3000 – Item Diagnostics

3001:	**TANAKH IN HEBREW, PRINTED IN FOUR VOLUMES** Ink on paper Hartford, Connecticut 1887 GC.BIB.002963.1-.4
3002:	**KING JAMES BIBLE, WITHOUT APOCRYPHA** Ink on paper Amsterdam, Netherlands 1679 GC.BIB.003666
3003:	**GENEVA BIBLE, WITHOUT APOCRYPHA (CONTRARY TO THE TABLE OF CONTENTS)** Ink on paper London, England 1599 GC.BIB.003468
3004:	**DOUAY-RHEIMS BIBLE, WITH 1546 DECREE FROM THE COUNCIL OF TRENT TRANSLATED INTO ENGLISH** Ink on paper New York, New York 1873 GC.BIB.002925
3005:	**DOUAY BIBLE, FIRST ROMAN CATHOLIC TRANSLATION OF THE OLD TESTAMENT INTO ENGLISH** Ink on paper Douai, France 1609–1610 GC.BIB.003631.2

Marcion's influence motivated other Christian leaders in the second century to discuss explicitly which writings their communities considered indispensable. They affirmed that the Church's worship and teaching were based on both (1) books inherited from ancient Israel (Genesis, Exodus, Leviticus, etc.) and (2) writings by Jesus' early followers, including four Gospels (Matthew, Mark, Luke, and John). Over time, they labeled these groupings as "Old Testament" and "New Testament" respectively. Naming both collections with the same noun affirmed the Church's belief that "The old and the new Testament show the same God…" (Item 3005). The contrasting adjectives indicate that these texts originated from two different periods in history. In the Roman Empire at this time, Christianity was viewed with suspicion as a recent development. By contrast, Judaism was respected for its antiquity, so the adjective "Old" initially evoked positive connotations.

The Jewish Tanakh   [Case 3100]

The Jewish Bible today is known as the Tanakh. This name is an acronym for its three collections: *Torah* (Law), *Nevi'im* (Prophets), and *Ketuvim* (Writings).

Scribes in ancient Israel, like many of their neighbors, copied their sacred literature on scrolls. Up to the present day, Jewish communities around the world have continued to use this traditional format to produce biblical manuscripts. The handwritten scrolls displayed here contain the entire Torah (Item 3102), less than half the Nevi'im (Items 3103, 3104, 3105), and a small fraction of the Ketuvim (Items 3106, 3107). As these examples demonstrate, it has never been customary or practical to fit the entire Tanakh on a single scroll. Storing books on multiple scrolls makes it easier to rearrange their sequence. By contrast, a printed codex—even a very small one—can contain all the books of the Tanakh and facilitate a standardized sequence (Item 3101).

The Torah and Nevi'im include the oldest books of the Bible. The Torah is comprised of the "five books of Moses," Genesis through Deuteronomy. The Nevi'im subdivides into two groups, each occupying four scrolls. The "Former Prophets" are Joshua, Judges, Samuel, and Kings. The "Latter Prophets" are Isaiah, Jeremiah, Ezekiel, and the Twelve (Hosea through Malachi). All of these books were originally written in Hebrew, the language of ancient Israel.

The Ketuvim encompass a variety of literature: three long collections of poetry (Psalms, Proverbs, and Job), five short scrolls read annually (Song of Songs, Ruth, Lamentations, Ecclesiastes, and Esther), the prophet Daniel, and histories from the Persian period (Ezra–Nehemiah and Chronicles). These books were also composed in Hebrew, with portions of Daniel and Ezra in Aramaic. Some, however, were not completed until the 300s–

100s BC, during the Hellenistic period, when Greek became the most widely used language in the Mediterranean world.

Judaism in Hellenistic and Roman times was diverse. Pharisees, Sadducees, Essenes, Zealots, Herodians, and other groups disagreed about major religious, political, and cultural issues. All Jews regarded the Torah as canonical. Its five books were the earliest to be translated into Greek. A few groups, such as the Samaritans and possibly the Sadducees, accepted only these five books as authoritative, but most Jewish communities had a larger canon. The Jews who preserved the Dead Sea Scrolls at Qumran collected all the books of the Tanakh, except possibly Esther, plus additional writings that they treated as similarly authoritative.

The Qumran community, like many Jewish voices in the New Testament (such as Jesus and Paul), usually summarized their sacred texts under two headings—"Moses and the prophets" or "the Law and the Prophets"—rather than three. The writings they reference as prophetic, however, include books from both the Nevi'im and Ketuvim.

Case 3100 – Item Diagnostics

3101:	MINIATURE TANAKH IN HEBREW Ink on paper Tel-Aviv, Israel 20th century GC.PBK.000777	3105:	SAMUEL SCROLL Ink on parchment Central Europe Late 19th or early 20th century GC.SCR.003556
3102:	TORAH SCROLL IN TIK Ink on parchment; wood, velvet, and silver Turkey or Greece; Israel 19th century; 20th century GC.SCR.001579, GC.ARK.000645.1-.3	3106:	CHRONICLES SCROLL Ink on parchment with wooden roller Poland 20th century GC.SCR.003549
3103:	ISAIAH SCROLL Ink on parchment Central Europe Late 19th or early 20th century GC.SCR.003553	3107:	ESTHER SCROLL Ink on gvil Israel 20th century GC.SCR.001069
3104:	SCROLL OF THE TWELVE MINOR PROPHETS Ink on parchment Central Europe Late 19th or early 20th century GC.SCR.003557		

The Christian Old Testament   [Case 3200]

Most differences between Christian canons today are found in the Old Testament. The Protestant Old Testament matches the Hebrew Tanakh in content (Item 3201). Catholic and Orthodox Bibles accept seven additional books: Tobit, Judith, 1-2 Maccabees, Wisdom of Solomon, Sirach, and Baruch, plus much longer versions of Esther and Daniel. Many of these texts were originally written in Hebrew or Aramaic, but they all survived through Greek and Latin translations (Items 3203, 3204). The Ethiopic canon is even larger. It includes ancient Jewish books that survive in no other modern biblical canon, such as Enoch "the prophet" (Item 3208). Other texts, including the Prayer of Manasseh (Item 3207), are found in Eastern Orthodox Bibles, too.

Case 3200 – Item Diagnostics

3201:	TANAKH IN HEBREW Ink on paper Frankfurt, Germany 1716 GC.BIB.000988	3205:	CORRESPONDENCE BETWEEN AUGUSTINE AND JEROME IN LATIN, SIGNED BY MARTIN LUTHER Ink on paper Germany or Italy 1523 GC.PBK.000190
3202:	LEAF FROM P. BODMER XXIV PSALMS 49-51 (XLVIII-L) IN GREEK Ink on papyrus Egypt 3rd–4th century AD GC.MS.000170.16	3206:	AUGUSTINE, *ENARRATIONES ON PSALMS 121-134 (CXX-CXXXIII)* Decorated manuscript on parchment Northern Italy, likely Milan Circa 1150–1175 GC.MS.000774
3203:	GREEK BIBLE, OLD AND NEW TESTAMENTS INK ON PAPER Frankfurt, Germany 1597 GC.BIB.001878.1	3207:	PSALTER IN GE'EZ, INCLUDING PSALM 151 AND PRAYER OF MANASSEH Decorated manuscript on parchment Ethiopia Early 20th century GC.MS.000305
3204:	VULGATE POCKET BIBLE WITH JEROME'S PROLOGUES Decorated manuscript on parchment Northern France or England Circa 13th century GC.MS.000343	3208:	THE BOOK OF ENOCH THE PROPHET Translated by Richard Laurence Ink on paper London, England 1892 GC.PBK.002221

The historical evidence for how these differences arose is complex. It includes ancient manuscripts, early canon lists, and how various texts were quoted or referenced as authoritative (Item 3202). From the 300s to the 1500s to the present day, scholars, religious leaders, and faith communities have debated how to interpret such evidence, and how to balance historical understanding with contemporary concerns.

In the first century AD, when Christianity was born, the sacred writings of Judaism circulated on multiple scrolls in both Hebrew and Greek. Jews in the early Church invited Gentiles (non-Jews) to worship Israel's God with them. They used Greek as a shared language. As their message spread throughout the Roman Empire, Christians lost contact with Hebrew but began translating their sacred texts from Greek into Latin. By the fourth century AD, Christians had numerous copies of Old Testament books in both Greek and Latin.

Around AD 390, the Christian scholar Jerome began retranslating the Old Testament into Latin from the original languages (Items 3204, 3201). While studying Hebrew and Aramaic with Jews in Palestine, Jerome noted that their canon had fewer books than the Greek Old Testament (Item 3203). Jerome labeled the books not found in the Palestinian Hebrew canon as "apocryphal," suggesting that they did not belong in the Bible.

Jerome's new project prompted another influential Christian leader, Augustine of Hippo, to write him several letters (Items 3205, 3206). Augustine's first letter begged Jerome to go back to making Latin translations from the Greek Old Testament ("the Septuagint") instead of relying on Hebrew. Augustine believed that the Septuagint was most trustworthy, because Christians had used it for over three centuries, and many thought its translators had been divinely inspired. The two men debated Hebrew versus Greek over several years. Each claimed that his views were supported by how New Testament authors quoted Old Testament texts (Item 3202). In the 1500s, their debate was renewed more sharply in disagreements between leaders of the Protestant Reformation and authorities in the Roman Catholic Church.

The Christian New Testament   [Case 3300]

The New Testament has twenty-seven books, all originally written in Greek. Its sequence roughly parallels that of the Old Testament. The collection begins with four Gospels as foundational narratives (Item 3301; compare five books of Moses). Next, Acts of the Apostles recounts the early formation of the community (Item 3302; compare Joshua, Judges, etc.). Thirdly, twenty-one epistles (letters) from early leaders—including Paul, James, Peter, John, and Jude—offer instruction for worship and wise living (Items 3304, 3005; compare Psalms, Proverbs, etc.). Lastly, the Book of Revelation, a.k.a. Apocalypse of John, concludes the collection with prophecy (Item 3303; compare Isaiah through Malachi).

Case 3300 – Item Diagnostics

3301:	P. BODMER XIV-XV (P75), FACSIMILE LUKE 24 – JOHN 1 Ink on papyrus Egypt 3rd century AD GC.FAC.000138.2 *Gift courtesy of the Vatican Apostolic Library, where the original manuscript is housed*	3304:	NEW TESTAMENT Translated by Nathan Scarlett Ink on paper London, England 1798 GC.BIB.003247
3302:	KING JAMES BIBLE Ink on paper New York, New York 1862 GC.BIB.000509	3305:	BIFOLIUM FROM P. BODMER VIII (P72), FACSIMILE 2 PETER 3 Ink on papyrus Egypt Late 3rd–early 4th century AD GC.FAC.000137.10
3303:	FEDERIGO DA VENEZIA, *COMMENTARY ON THE APOCALYPSE* Illuminated manuscript on parchment Venice, Italy Circa 1420 GC.MS.000483	3306:	LUTHER NEW TESTAMENT Translated by Martin Luther Ink on paper Wittenberg, Germany 1524 GC.BIB.003839

As a whole, this list was settled in the late 300s at official meetings such as the Council of Laodicea in AD 363 and the Synod of Hippo in AD 393. Delegates from various regions gathered to discuss issues relevant to the entire Church. Much of the New Testament canon had formed earlier. Two smaller collections—the four Gospels (Matthew, Mark, Luke, John) and the Pauline Epistles (Romans through Philemon)—were widely used from the 100s onward. Acts, 1 Peter, and 1 John were also already widely accepted. A few books, however, were still debated: six epistles (Hebrews, James, 2 Peter, 2-3 John, and Jude) plus the Book of Revelation.

Four criteria were cited as tests for canonical status: apostolicity, orthodoxy (fitting with already accepted books), widespread use, and antiquity. Apostolicity meant that a book either was written by an apostle (a first-generation follower directly commissioned by Jesus, such as Matthew, John, Peter, and Paul) or directly transmitted an apostle's teaching (for example, Mark and Luke were remembered as coworkers of Peter and Paul, respectively).

In the late 300s, the most debated books were Hebrews and Revelation. Hebrews was problematic because of its anonymity. Eastern churches thought it was written by Paul and used it. Western churches did not. This letter's position in the canon today, following Philemon, demonstrates their compromise (Item 3304). The Book of Revelation was controversial because Eastern churches worried that its visions were read too literally. It gained acceptance by being interpreted allegorically, satisfying the criterion of orthodoxy (Item 3303).

The Syriac New Testament, translated around the early 400s, had only twenty-two books. The absence of 2 Peter (Item 3305), 2-3 John, Jude, and Revelation initially reflected timing rather than controversy. Through contact with other churches, West Syrians added these books in the 500s-600s AD. Controversies about other issues separated East Syrians from this development.

In the 1500s, Martin Luther argued that four previously debated books—Hebrews, James, Jude, and Revelation—did not adequately "preach Christ." His New Testament translation segregated these books at the end (Item 3306). Their long-established canonical status, however, stopped Luther from omitting them entirely.

The Reformation Theatre (Video)

The Reformation Theatre gives us a front-row seat to a hypothetical debate between three intellectual giants of sixteenth-century Christianity—Martin Luther, Desiderius Erasmus, and Johann Eck—as they discuss the greatest controversy of their day, the Protestant Reformation. At the center is a young priest named Martin Luther, who was extremely critical of the Church, eventually encouraging people to break with the authority of Rome. To Luther's right (the viewer's left) is the scholar Desiderius Erasmus, who criticized some of the Church's practices in his book *In Praise of Folly*, but who remained faithful to the Church throughout his lifetime. On Luther's left (the viewer's right) is Johann Eck, a staunch supporter of Rome and a defender of the Pope, who opposed Luther both in debate at Leipzig (1519) and at the imperial investigation of Luther at Worms (1521).

Over the course of this presentation, these three men debate the core issues of the Protestant Reformation:

- Whether the Christian faith is based solely on scripture or upon the three-fold authorities of scripture, tradition, and the Church Magisterium
- Whether a person is justified by faith alone or through a combination of faith and deeds
- What role the vernacular, or common, language should have in relation to the Bible and the liturgy

Martin Luther's view on these issues led him to create a list of grievances with the Catholic Church and several of its practices. Legend says that Luther nailed his "95 Theses" to the door of the Castle Church in Wittenberg, Germany, on October 31, 1517—an act often cited as the beginning of the Protestant Reformation.

Just beyond this theatre is a room containing original writings from Luther, Erasmus, Eck, and others involved in the Protestant Reformation.

Martin Luther: Protest, Reform, and Excommunication   [Case 3400]
Martin Luther was born in Eisleben, Germany, on November 10, 1483. As a young man, he studied to become a lawyer, but he left university at the age of 21 to become an Augustinian friar.

Case 3400 – Item Diagnostics

3401:	**MARTIN LUTHER, SIGNED LETTER** Ink on paper Nuremberg, Germany October 4, 1518 GC.PPR.000115
3402:	**MARTIN LUTHER, *AGAINST HENRY, KING OF THE ENGLISH*** (Response to Henry VIII's condemnation of Luther's *Babylonian Captivity of the Church*) Ink on paper Wittenberg, Germany 1522 GC.PBK.000371
3403:	**MARTIN LUTHER, "AVOIDING THE DOCTRINES OF MEN"** Ink on paper Wittenberg, Germany 1522 GC.PAM.000161
3404:	**POPE LEO X, *BULL AGAINST THE ERRORS OF MARTIN LUTHER*** Published by Andreas Lutz Ingolstadt, Bavaria 1520 GC.PBK.000243
3405:	**POPE ADRIAN VI, *BRIEF OF POPE ADRIAN VI AGAINST LUTHER*** Ink on paper Wittenberg, Germany November 30, 1523 GC.PBK.000242

In 1510, Luther traveled to Rome, Italy, where he became frustrated by the corruption he felt was present among the clergy. He particularly disagreed with the sale of indulgences, which the Church was conducting to raise money for building St. Peter's Basilica in Rome. When a person bought an "indulgence," it supposedly reduced the amount of time they spent in Purgatory—the realm of the afterlife before Heaven, where souls did penance for the sins they had committed in life. In 1517, after Pope Leo X ordered a new round of indulgences to be sold, Luther became so angry that he wrote a treatise outlining his complaints against the Catholic Church—his "95 Theses." Less than a year later, he was summoned to Augsburg, where the papal legate, Cardinal Cajetan, on charges of heresy, interviewed him. On October 6, 1518, just six days before meeting with the cardinal, he wrote a letter giving much insight into his thoughts (Item 3401). In it he says, "Let the Lord's will be done. [...] For Jesus Christ is in control both in Augsburg and in the midst of His enemies."

At Augsburg, Luther refused to retract his statements condemning the Church. Instead, he continued to write and to speak publicly about his criticisms of the Catholic Church, publishing books like the *Babylonian Captivity of the Church*, which caused him to enter into debate with King Henry VIII of England (Item 3402). Finally, in June 1520, Pope Leo X issued a papal decree denouncing Martin Luther's claims as being "against the doctrine and tradition of the Catholic Church, and against the true interpretation of the sacred Scriptures received from the Church" (Item 3404). Pope Leo X demanded that Luther repent and recant within 60 days. If he did not, he would be excommunicated and would face execution as a heretic. Luther responded by publicly burning the bull six months later, on December 10, 1520, in Wittenberg.

He was excommunicated officially on January 3, 1521, by the Edict of Worms, which forced him into hiding for a number of years. While in hiding, he continued publishing books and pamphlets, such as his 1522 essay "Avoiding the Doctrines of Men" (Item 3403). As a result, on November 30, 1522, Pope Adrian VI released another papal decree condemning Luther and his followers (Item 3405). For the rest of his life, Luther continued to work for reform and drew many to his ideas.

Biblical Scholarship and the Reformation   [Case 3500]

Throughout the Middle Ages, Latin had been the primary biblical language in Europe, and any translations that were made used the Latin Vulgate as their base text. In the Early Modern period, however, biblical scholarship focused on a return to the original languages of the Bible. This return was particularly favored by the Reformers,

Case 3500 – Item Diagnostics

3501:	**DESIDERIUS ERASMUS,** *COMMENTARY ON PARAPHRASE OF THE LATIN NEW TESTAMENT* Ink on paper Basel, Switzerland 1522 GC.PBK.000194
3502:	**DESIDERIUS ERASMUS,** *GREEK NEW TESTAMENT,* **FIRST OCTAVO EDITION** Printed by Johann Froben Ink on paper Basel, Switzerland 1521 GC.BIB.001155
3503:	**DESIDERIUS ERASMUS,** *NOTES ON THE NEW TESTAMENT* Ink on parchment Basel, Switzerland 1519 GC.PBK.002292
3504:	**COMPLUTENSIAN POLYGLOT, VOLUME V: NEW TESTAMENT** Ink on paper Alcalá de Henares, Spain 1514–1517 GC.BIB.001428.5
3505:	**DANIEL BOMBERG, OLD TESTAMENT IN HEBREW, VOLUME I: PENTATEUCH** Ink on paper Italy 1525–1526 GC.BIB.003057.1

who thought that the Vulgate translation was untrue to the original intent of the Bible and was being used by the Church to promote its own agenda.

In the first decades of the sixteenth century, a group of Catholic scholars at the University of Complutense in Spain produced the first complete polyglot Bible: the Complutensian Polyglot (Item 3504). Made up of six volumes, this book allowed readers to compare the Latin text of the Bible with the original languages in which it was written—Hebrew, Aramaic, and Greek. The Complutensian Polyglot was of enormous value to early Bible translators, providing access to the Bible in the original languages, the text of some of the earliest biblical translations, with extensive notes and study aids—all in one work.

Around the same time, a Dutch priest named Desiderius Erasmus embarked on a similar task. In 1516, he produced the first published version of the New Testament in Greek. The publisher even secured an exclusive four-year publishing privilege from Holy Roman Emperor Maximilian I and Pope Leo X. This meant publication of the Complutensian Polyglot was delayed until 1520-22, even though it was finished in 1514. Erasmus's text was extremely popular with scholars and was reprinted numerous times (Items 3502, 3503). His second edition even formed the base for Martin Luther's German translation of the New Testament.

Erasmus also produced his own Latin paraphrase of the New Testament, as well as a commentary on this translation (Item 3501). This was seen by many as a condemnation of the Latin Vulgate. Nevertheless, Erasmus remained Catholic for the rest of his life. Like Luther, he believed that people should have access to the Bible in their own language. He disagreed with Luther's interpretations of the Bible, however, as well as with Luther's decision to cause division within the Church.

Luther's German Bible and the Catholic Response   [Case 3600]

Between May 1521 and April 1522, Martin Luther lived in hiding in Wartburg Castle. When Pope Leo X excommunicated him from the Church, Luther was considered an outlaw. However, he had gained a powerful supporter—Frederick III, Elector of Saxony—who secretly arranged Luther's safe travel to the castle after his examination by Johann Eck at Worms. As a disguise, he grew a beard and called himself "Knight George." While living there, Luther produced his German translation of the New Testament (Item 3601). It was a difficult and lonely time. Later in life, Luther stated that he was frequently plagued by the devil during those months, but that he had "driven him away with his ink." Though he was likely referring to the process of translation, one legend says that Luther literally threw his inkpot across the room to chase away the devil!

Once it was safe for Luther to come out of hiding, he worked with his friend Philip Melanchthon to correct the manuscript and get it published. Then, he started work on a multi-volume translation of the Old Testament (Item 3602). By this time, he no longer worked alone, but had gathered a committee of talented men who worked together to develop the text.

Luther's translation was extremely controversial, as he used it to further his own theological readings of the biblical text. For example, based on his doctrine of justification, he inserted the word "alone" (or "*allein,*" in German) after "faith" in Romans 3:28. Luther insisted that his addition was justified, as it was implied in the Greek text. This and other "Protestant" phrases encouraged the Catholic Church scholar Jerome Esmer to produce his own translation of the New Testament into German (Item 3603). Published in 1527, Esmer's text actually drew heavily from Luther's German, but he made a number of changes to bring the text back in line with the Vulgate.

Despite this and other rival translations, Luther's German Bible gained widespread popularity, and remained the most important Bible translation in Germany for hundreds of years.

Case 3600 – Item Diagnostics

3601:	MARTIN LUTHER, NEW TESTAMENT IN GERMAN	3603:	JEROME ESMER, CATHOLIC TRANSLATION OF THE NEW TESTAMENT IN GERMAN
	Printed by Melchior Lotter		Printed by Wolfgang Stockel
	Ink and pigment on paper		Dresden, Germany
	Wittenberg, Germany		1527
	1524		GC.BIB.000688
	GC.BIB.002619		
3602:	MARTIN LUTHER, OLD TESTAMENT IN GERMAN, VOLUME II	3604:	ORDINATION CERTIFICATE, SIGNED BY MARTIN LUTHER
	Ink on paper		Ink on paper
	Wittenberg, Germany		Wittenberg, Germany
	1524		March 19, 1544
	On loan from a private collection		GC.ART.001155

Global Effects: Northern Europe, England, and the Counter-Reformation   [Case 3700]

The effects of the Reformation spread quickly throughout Europe, taking hold in Germany, Scandinavia, Switzerland, and elsewhere. Though Luther's ideas formed the basis of the widespread Protestantism, other theologians soon came onto the scene. Some of the most well-known are Ulrich Zwingli and John Calvin, both of whom were influential in the foundation of the Reformed denominations.

In England, Luther's ideas gained a lot of popularity among the university crowd. Cambridge, in particular, latched onto the new Protestant theology, and people there began meeting at a local pub to discuss the works of Luther and the other Humanists. Though these men were scholars reading Luther's writings in their original Latin, his works were later translated into English for a more popular audience (Item 3702).

One of the central figures of the English Reformation was Thomas Cranmer. As a scholar at Cambridge, he had read the works of both Luther and Erasmus, whom he particularly admired. Cranmer was Archbishop of Canterbury during the English Church's split from Rome, and a strong advocate of doctrinal reform within the Church of England. Though the English Reformation differed from its Continental counterparts in many respects, certain similarities—such as conducting services in the vernacular, an emphasis on justification by faith, and the right of priests to get married—owe a great deal to Cranmer. When Queen Mary I took control of England, she returned the country to Catholicism. As a result, Cranmer was charged with heresy, imprisoned at Oxford, and finally burned at the stake on March 21, 1556 (Item 3701). He and his fellow reformers Hugh Latimer and Nicholas Ridley are known as the Oxford Martyrs.

Case 3700 – Item Diagnostics

3701:	JOHN FOXE, *THE BOOK OF MARTYRS*, VOLUME III Ink on paper London, England 1631–1641 GC.PBK.001472.3
3702:	MARTIN LUTHER, *COMMENTARY... UPON THE EPISTLE OF S. PAUL TO THE GALATIANS* Printed by Thomas Vautrollier London, England 1580 GC.PBK.000196
3703:	POPE PAUL III, PAPAL BULL Ink on parchment Rome, Italy August 1543

With the Reformation sweeping across Europe, the Catholic Church responded in several ways. The Catholic Reformation, often called the Counter-Reformation, was a period of reform and renewal (1560-1648) that took place within the Catholic Church to address the issues and concerns highlighted by the Protestant Reformers. One of the major events of the Counter-Reformation was the Council of Trent (1545-1563), called by Pope Leo III (Item 3703). The Council upheld the Catholic position on the sacraments and on salvation through faith and works. It decreed the importance of the Vulgate, rejecting Bible translation by Protestants. The Counter-Reformation also emphasized the importance of educating priests and lay people about the theology and practices of the church. New religious orders, such as the Jesuits and Capuchins, were created to bring about a genuine renewal of spirituality in the Church. Finally, a renewed emphasis was placed on having a personal relationship with Jesus Christ, as seen in the writings of Spanish mystics like Teresa of Avila and John of the Cross.

The Bible and Slavery

The practice of slavery in various cultures has been recorded and documented for thousands of years. Some of our earliest writings on cuneiform tablets maintain records of slave ownership. The famous Code of Hammurabi, composed in Babylon around 1750 BC, indicates that criminal punishments were partially determined based on the status—slave or free man—of the victim and perpetrator.

Slavery is documented in almost every ancient civilization: Sumer, Egypt, China, Assyria, Babylonia, India, Greece, the Roman Empire, the Islamic Caliphate, Israel, and the pre-Columbian civilizations of the Americas. The Bible recognized slavery as an established institution, and it was, for the most part, an inherent practice of the day.

Although slavery has been documented in pre-Columbian civilizations, the ascension of the transatlantic slave trade in the Americas begin during the reign of King Ferdinand II of Aragon and Queen Isabella I of Castile, following Christopher Columbus's second expedition in 1493. The Spanish inquisition forced thousands of indigenous Americans into gold and silver mines, and onto cocoa, sugar, coffee, tobacco, and cotton plantations. In the sixteenth century, captive West Africans began to be transported as slaves to the shores of North and South America. It has been estimated that approximately 12 million Africans sailed across the Atlantic and were sold into slavery before the practice was finally abolished.

The Bible has been used both to justify and to condemn slavery. Ultimately, it can be argued that the Bible and its followers were among the most important and instrumental influences in the abolishment of slavery in both Europe and the Americas.

Slavery: A History of Oppression   [Case 3800]

Slavery has been present from earliest recorded history. Item 3801 is a cuneiform tablet that records a legal dispute involving a slave accused of stealing barley from his owner, a man of status or wealth. The witnesses to the case were of esteemed positions: court envoys, two sons of the king and a court singer. It is assumed from the text that the defendant was sentenced to a longer duration of servitude for his crime.

Case 3800 – Item Diagnostics

3801:	**CUNEIFORM TABLET** Court summary of case involving Mesopotamian slave Clay Southern Iraq Circa 2050 BC GC.CUN.000242
3802:	**BARTOLOMÉ DE LAS CASAS, *A SHORT ACCOUNT OF THE DESTRUCTION OF THE INDIES*, FIRST EDITION** Printed by Sebastian Trugillo Ink on paper Seville, Spain 1552–1553 *From the Collection of Dr. and Mrs. R. Ted Steinbock*
3803:	**JOSIAH PRIEST, *BIBLE DEFENSE OF SLAVERY*** Printed by W.S. Brown Ink on paper Glasgow, Kentucky 1851 GC.PBK.001470

European-enforced slavery in the Americas began when sixteenth-century Spanish colonists enslaved the indigenous people, sending them to work in mines or on plantations. Bartolomé de las Casas—a Spanish Dominican Friar and missionary to the Americas—spoke out against these practices (Item 3802). He exposed the atrocities and oppression placed upon the indigenous people of the West Indies by the Spanish crown. His most notable works, *A Short Account of the Destruction of the Indies* and *General History of the Indies*, depict the European colonization of the West Indies and their inhumane treatment of its indigenous people. His extensive writings for the fair treatment of the Native Americans earned him the official title as "Protector of the Indians."

In 1550, King Charles called a royal council to hear a formal debate on the question "Is it lawful for the king of Spain to wage war on the Indians?" Renowned Spanish philosopher Juan Ginés de Sepúlveda argued that it was, while Bartolomé de las Casas argued that it was not. In defending the rights of the indigenous Americans, De las Casas referenced multiple passages from the Bible, including Romans 10, Exodus 10, Hebrews 2, 1 Corinthians 15, and Philippians 3.

In the nineteenth century, people again turned to the Bible to address the topic of slavery, though not always to oppose it. In 1843, Josiah Priest wrote a book called *Slavery, As It Relates to the Negro, Of African Race*, later republished as *Bible Defense of Slavery* (Item 3803). In his text, Priest assembles a collection of proslavery literature and propaganda to support the institution of slavery in the United States. His opening preface states,

> *If [slavery] be in harmony with the immutable principles of truth and justice, and not a 'crime against humanity,' and a libel upon our holy religion, let it be so understood and practiced by our honest citizens, whose highest ambition consists in faithfully serving God, and living in obedience to the laws of the country.*

His conclusion—that the "appointment of this race of men to servitude and slavery, was a judicial act of God, or in other words was a divine judgment"—was popular throughout the South prior to the Civil War.

Transatlantic Slave Trade   [Case 3900]

For 300 years, the transatlantic slave trade transported roughly 12 million Africans as slaves across the Atlantic Ocean to the Americas. Confined by shackles (Item 3901) and crammed into boats several hundred at a time, many individuals did not survive the journey across the "Middle Passage" from Africa to the Americas.

From the sixteenth to the eighteenth centuries, Spain, Portugal, France, Denmark, and England and their colonies all participated in the slave trade. Some slave-traders captured and enslaved Africans themselves, while others bought their slaves from members of other African tribes in exchange for some token. Bracelets made of copper or bronze were commonly used for this purpose (Item 3902). Copper was the "red gold" of Africa. The Portuguese explorer Duatre Pacheco Pereire wrote about this practice in the early sixteenth century after a visit to Benin, Africa, saying that the country "is usually at war with its neighbors and takes many captives, whom we buy at twelve or fifteen brass bracelets each, or for copper bracelets, which they prize more."

In Europe, there were many who disapproved of the horrors of slavery and fought for its abolition. In 1785, Cambridge University held an essay competition with the title: "Is it right to make men slaves against their wills?" A young man named Thomas Clarkson won first prize with his essay, and was asked to read it to the University Senate (Item 3903). On his way home to London, he experienced what he later described as a divine revelation ordering him to devote his life to abolishing slavery.

Together with the lawyer Granville Sharp and ten others, Clarkson formed the Society for the Abolition of the

Case 3900 – Item Diagnostics

3901:	SHACKLES FROM BEDFORD COUNTY JAIL	3903:	THOMAS CLARKSON, *AN ESSAY ON THE SLAVERY AND COMMERCE OF THE HUMAN SPECIES*
	Cast iron		Printed by Joseph Crukshank
	England		Ink on paper
	17th century		Philadelphia, Pennsylvania
	Loan courtesy of Andrew Stimer		1786
			From the Collection of Dr. and Mrs. R. Ted Steinbock
3902:	AFRICAN SLAVE BRACELETS	3904:	PORTION OF AN ACT FOR THE ABOLITION OF THE SLAVE TRADE, PUBLISHED IN *THE LONDON GAZETTE*
	Bronze		Ink on paper
	Europe		London, England
	17th century		1807
	GC.JWL.000136, GC.JWL.000137		GC.PPR.010222

Slave Trade in May 1787. Nine of the committee members were Quakers, and the society gained the support of important figures like John Wesley and Josiah Wedgwood. Later they persuaded William Wilberforce, a Member of Parliament, to present their cause to the House of Commons. Clarkson collected the evidence to support their case, interviewing an estimated 20,000 sailors and gathering examples of the tools used on slave-ships, including handcuffs, leg shackles, thumbscrews, and branding irons.

In 1807, Britain passed *An Act for the Abolition of the Slave Trade*, which made the slave trade illegal throughout the British Empire (Item 3904). This Act imposed fines on those who continued to engage in the elicit act of slave trade. From 1808 to 1860, it is estimated that the Royal Navy seized over 1,500 slave ships and rescued 150,000 Africans. Anti-slavery agreements and treaties were signed with African leaders. America followed suit, but still allowed slave trading within the confines of the United States borders. In 1833, the Slavery Abolition Act was passed in Britain, encompassing the entire British Empire.

Voices of Freedom and Justice   [Case 4000]

The Clapham Sect, also known as the Clapham Saints, was a group of prominent British Anglican leaders, based in London at the beginning of the nineteenth century, who used their influence to promote morality, Christian values, and social reforms. Many of the "Claphamites" were Members of Parliament. The most influential and outspoken of its leaders was William Wilberforce, a politician, philanthropist, and influential leader in the British abolitionist movement (Items 4001, 4002). Wilberforce relentlessly presented the matter of slavery before the House of Commons, until he won the support of the majority in abolishing slavery throughout the British Empire.

Another member of the Clapham Sect was poet and writer Hannah More (Item 4003). Through her writings, she provided a public voice, alongside Wilberforce's, to the plight of the African slave trade. In 1788, she published "Slavery, A Poem," in which she questions why Liberty's light only shines on some people and not others. That same year, More republished "The Sorrows of Yamba, or The Negro Woman's Lamentation." The poem presents the story of Yamba, a slave woman who is ripped from her home and her family, and sent to work in the West Indies. The poem was a call to arms for the abolitionist movement. In one of the final stanzas, More implores,

Case 4000 – Item Diagnostics

4001:	ABSTRACT OF LAND DONATED TO THE ABOLITIONIST CAUSE, SIGNED BY WILLIAM WILBERFORCE Ink on Paper London, England 1803 GC.PPR.010223	4003:	HANNAH MORE, *THE WORKS OF HANNAH MORE: STORIES FOR THE PERSONS IN THE MIDDLE RANKS* Published by H. Fisher and P. Jackson Ink on paper London, England 1836 GC.PBK.000648.1-.6
4002:	WILLIAM WILBERFORCE, *AN APPEAL TO THE RELIGION, JUSTICE, AND HUMANITY... IN BEHALF OF THE NEGRO SLAVES IN THE WEST INDIES*, SIGNED BY AUTHOR Printed by J. Hatchard and Son Ink on paper London, England 1823 GC.PBK.002294	4004:	KING JAMES BIBLE, CONTAINING SIX STANZA POEM "PRECIOUS BIBLE," HANDWRITTEN BY JOHN NEWTON Oxford, England Ink on paper 1774 GC.BIB.000306

Cease, ye British Sons of murder!
Cease from forging Afric's Chain;
Mock your Saviour's name no further,
Cease your savage lust of gain.

Both William Wilberforce and Hannah More received spiritual counsel from an Anglican priest named John Newton (Item 4004). Newton, best known as the author of "Amazing Grace," was a former slave trader. Newton's influence on Wilberforce had a considerable impact. Wilberforce considered leaving politics for the ministry, but Newton encouraged him to stay in Parliament and "serve God where he was." Newton's advice provided Wilberforce with "increased diligence and conscientiousness" as he faced criticism from his peers in the House of Commons for his unrelenting stance on the issues of slavery.

In large part because of the efforts of the Clapham Sect, the Slave Trade Act was passed in 1807, marking the beginning of the end of the Atlantic slave trade.

Case 4100 – Item Diagnostics

4101:	**ANTHONY BENEZET, *A CAUTION AND WARNING... OF THE CALAMITOUS STATE OF THE ENSLAVED NEGROES IN THE BRITISH DOMINIONS*** Published by D. Hall and W. Sellers Ink on paper Philadelphia, Pennsylvania 1767 *From the Collection of Dr. and Mrs. R. Ted Steinbock*
4102:	**JONATHAN EDWARDS, *THE INJUSTICE AND IMPOLICY OF THE SLAVE TRADE*** Sermon preached before the Connecticut Society for the Promotion of Freedom Printed by Thomas and Samuel Green Ink on paper New Haven, Connecticut September 15, 1791 *From the Collection of Dr. and Mrs. R. Ted Steinbock*
4103:	**SLAVE TRADE ACT, PUBLISHED IN THE *COLUMBIAN CENTINEL*** Printed by Benjamin Russell Ink on paper Boston, Massachusetts 1794 *Loan courtesy of Andrew Stimer*
4104:	**DEED TO A SLAVE** Ink on paper Washington, DC 1878 GC.PPR.010224
4105:	**SLAVE TAG** Copper Charleston, South Carolina 1830 *Loan courtesy of Andrew Stimer*

Slavery in the United States of America [Case 4100]

In 1767, Pennsylvanian abolitionist Anthony Benezet wrote an essay entitled, *A caution and warning to Great Britain, and her colonies, in a short representation of the calamitous state of the enslaved Negroes in the British dominions* (Item 4101). This famous appeal for the liberty and better treatment of the Negro was made to the American colonies when they were beginning to seek their own liberty from Britain. Benezet hoped to capitalize on this spirit of revolution in his efforts to secure the freedom of enslaved African Americans. In his text, he cites the "golden rule," found in Luke 6:31, in support of abolition. Benezet is credited with founding the world's first abolition society, "The Society for the Relief of Free Negroes Unlawfully Held in Bondage," on April 14, 1775, in Philadelphia, Pennsylvania.

Connecticut theologian Jonathan Edwards, notable for the role he played in the Great Awakening in New England, also supported the abolition movement. In 1791, he preached a sermon to a local anti-slavery group in which he notes that abolition was gaining support in the North and predicts that in fifty years slavery would be over (Item 4102). Edwards echoes Anthony Benezet's use of the "golden rule" and the philosophies of the Revolutionary era to justify the abolition of slavery.

Item 4103 is a news report in the *Columbian Centinel*—published in Boston, MA—on five early acts of the U.S. Congress, all signed in script type by President George Washington. The most significant of these was the Slave Trade Act, passed in 1794. This action of Congress is viewed as the official beginning of the American abolitionist movement.

Even though the slave trade had been abolished, slavery itself was still practiced within the United States. The 1818 document shown here (Item 4104) records the sale of a slave in Washington, DC, by Charles Belt, the owner of the Chevy Chase Plantation. In it, Belt sells "a certain negro named Charles" for $700. It was witnessed by Thomas Corcoran, former mayor of Georgetown. This underscores the fact that slaves were treated as property, bought and sold as any commodity.

Item 4105 is a stamped copper tag made in Charleston, SC, in 1830, with the word SERVANT in capital letters across the width of the tag. The number 1750 presumably identifies a particular slave. This piece was unearthed in 1990.

The American Civil War   [Case 4200]

The American Civil War began in January 1861, when seven southern states seceded from the Union to form the Confederate States of America. One of the main points of disagreement between the North and the South that led to that moment was the issue of slavery.

When Abraham Lincoln met Harriet Beecher Stowe, the author of *Uncle Tom's Cabin*, in 1862, he reportedly greeted her saying, "So you're the little woman who wrote the book that made this great war." In the emotionally charged atmosphere of mid-nineteenth-century America, *Uncle Tom's Cabin* exploded like a bombshell as it outlined the atrocities committed against the African slave (Item 4201). In her novel, Stowe tries to demonstrate that the system of slavery and the moral code of Christianity oppose each other. Historians argue that Stowe's work changed the course of history, igniting the spark that started the Civil War. *Uncle Tom's Cabin* was the second best-selling book of the nineteenth century, following the Bible. It is one of the most socially influential American books ever published.

In 1862, the year after the Confederacy seceded from the Union, the Confederate States Bible Society issued its first New Testament imprint (Item 4202). The South was unable to import Bibles from the British and Foreign Bible Societies due to Union blockades, so they decided to print their own. They were designed to be small enough to fit into a soldier's pocket, so that he could take the Bible into

Case 4200 – Item Diagnostics

4201:	**HARRIET BEECHER STOWE, *UNCLE TOM'S CABIN*, FIRST EDITION** Published by John P. Jewett and Company Ink on paper Boston, Massachusetts 1852 *From the Collection of Dr. and Mrs. R. Ted Steinbock*
4202:	**CONFEDERATE STATES NEW TESTAMENT, FIRST EDITION** Published by Confederate States Bible Society Printed by Wood, Hanleiter Rice and Company Ink on paper Atlanta, Georgia 1862 GC.BIB.001438
4203:	**LEVI COFFIN, *REMINISCENCES OF LEVI COFFIN, THE REPUTED PRESIDENT OF THE UNDERGROUND RAILROAD*** Published by Western Tract Society Ink on paper Cincinnati, Ohio 1876 *From the Collection of Dr. and Mrs. R. Ted Steinbock*

battle with him. Issued with paper wraps, few of these New Testaments survived the brutal conflict of the Civil War.

In the years leading up to the Civil War, one of the primary ways that slaves escaped from the South was through the Underground Railroad—a system of secret routes and safe points leading to the northern states. One of the most important people involved in that movement was Levi Coffin, a Quaker who was part of the Underground Railroad in Indiana and Ohio. Before he died, he wrote a memoir about his experiences (Item 4203). Coffin was nicknamed "President of the Underground Railroad," because he helped so many slaves to safety, and his home was often called the "Grand Central Station of the Underground Railroad." Coffin was so successful that, while he was in Newport, not a single slave failed to reach freedom. One of the many slaves who hid in the Coffin home was Eliza Harris, whose story Harriet Beecher Stowe—a friend of the Coffins—told in *Uncle Tom's Cabin*.

The Emancipation Proclamation and the Gettysburg Address   [Case 4300]

Following the election of Abraham Lincoln in 1860, America was emotionally charged with concerns over issues of state's rights, slavery, and the abolitionist movement. During this time, Lincoln was primarily concerned with keeping the Union together. Although he was a staunch advocate of the abolitionist movement, he had previously stated that he would not interfere with slavery where it already existed.

In 1862, Lincoln issued a preliminary Emancipation Proclamation as a strategic war maneuver. He warned that, if the southern states did not cease their dissent, the Proclamation would go into effect. After the North's victory at the Battle of Antietam, Lincoln felt that the government had proven its ability to enforce the Emancipation Proclamation. In 1863, President Lincoln issued the Emancipation Proclamation, which declared, "that all persons held as slaves within the rebellious states are, and henceforward shall be free" (Item 4301).

Following the Emancipation Proclamation, further advancement of every federal troop expanded the quest for freedom. The Proclamation itself announced the acceptance of black men into the Union Army and Navy, assisting those that were once shackled to sever the ties that once bound them. By the end of the war, over 150,000 black soldiers and sailors had fought for the Union and freedom (Item 4303).

During the dedication of the Soldiers' National Cemetery in Gettysburg, Pennsylvania, a few months after Union soldiers had defeated the Confederacy, both at Antietam and Gettysburg, Lincoln gave what would become one of the best-known speeches in American history: the Gettysburg Address (Item 4302). In this short speech, Lincoln reiterated the principles of America's founding document, that all

Case 4300 – Item Diagnostics

4301:	ABRAHAM LINCOLN, *THE EMANCIPATION PROCLAMATION* Printed by the Government Printing Office Ink on paper Washington, DC 1863 *From the Collection of Dr. and Mrs. R. Ted Steinbock*
4302:	ABRAHAM LINCOLN, *THE GETTYSBURG ADDRESS* Published by Singerly & Myers, State Printers Ink on paper Harrisburg, Pennsylvania 1864 *From the Collection of Dr. and Mrs. R. Ted Steinbock*
4303:	BIBLE AND PERSONAL EFFECTS BELONGING TO PRIVATE GEORGE R. ROME Various materials United States 1864–1889 GC.PPR.009947, GC.BIB.003796, GC.ART.001146, GC.OBJ.000336.1-.4, GC.OBJ.000334.1-.3

men are created equal. He completed his two minute speech by saying, "We here highly resolve that these dead shall not have died in vain—that this nation, under God, shall have a new birth of freedom—and that government of the people, by the people, for the people, shall not perish from the earth." The Gettysburg Address redefined the Civil War as a struggle not just for the Union, but also for the principle of human equality.

Jewish Persecution: Pre-Holocaust Pogroms

Pogroms are coordinated acts of violence against a specific ethnic group, typically targeting Jews and other minority groups. These aggressions often result in the displacement of indigenous communities, bloodshed, and, in the worst instances, the attempted eradication of entire populations. The Armenian Genocide and the German Holocaust are two of the most memorable pogroms in modern history.

For understanding the current state of Jewish diaspora in the modern world, these displays focus on pogroms that resulted in the displacement of Jewish communities from the late fifteenth century onward.

Treatment of Jews during the Spanish Inquisition   [Case 4400]

The current state of diaspora for Spanish Jews is due in part to natural migrations from fluctuating socio-economic conditions. A pivotal event occurred at the turn of the fifteenth century, however, just one century after the riots of 1391 in which thousands of Spanish Jews were slaughtered. The Spanish Inquisition, commissioned to root out heretics, resulted in the expulsion of tens of thousands of Jews and Muslims who resisted conversion to Christianity, or who became *conversos*, and were still perceived as threats to the Spanish—and staunchly Catholic—crown.

Case 4400 – Item Diagnostics

4401:	ROYAL DOCUMENT, SIGNED "LA REYNA" BY ISABELLA I, QUEEN OF SPAIN Handwritten on paper Seville, Spain 1500 GC.PPR.010221
4402:	INQUISITION ERA SCROLL Ink on gvil Spain 15th century GC.SCR.000769

Ferdinand II and Isabella I were the ruling monarchs responsible for the formation of the tribunal that saw to the proceedings of the Inquisition. Item 4401 is an original letter signed by Queen Isabella in which she references the Jewish and Muslim *conversos*. It also mentions Gabriel Sánchez, a prominent courtier from a family of known Jewish *conversos*, who served as treasurer to the king. Of the Jews who resisted conversion, many were forcibly expelled or voluntarily immigrated to northern Africa, both settling in established communities and founding new centers of Jewish culture across the Maghreb, including Morocco, Algeria, and Tunisia. This displacement would also result in a Jewish presence in the "New World", in such countries as Argentina, Cuba and elsewhere.

These communities originating from *sfarad*, or Spain, culturally identify as *sephardim*. The Torah scroll (Item 4402) is an example of the rich Sephardic culture which thrived in Spain, prior to the Inquisition. It is believed to have originated from Spain, and was probably commissioned sometime around the last half of the fifteenth century. Scrolls, which were produced in subsequent years, demonstrating Spanish influence, have been found throughout North Africa, and serve as a testament to the survival of the Sephardic scribal school and culture.

In February of 2014, the Spanish Ministry of Justice issued a formal apology to the descendants of all

Sephardic Jews, granting Spanish nationality to any qualifying individuals wishing to return—allowing for potentially hundreds of thousands of people to become documented EU citizens.

Pogroms of the Middle East and Western Asia   [Case 4500]

Jewish communities have populated areas of the Middle East and parts of Central Asia for thousands of years—most notably within those territories of modern Iraq. Historically, the "Babylonian" Jews are one of the better-documented demographics of the region. For over two and a half millennia, Mesopotamia (modern Iraq) would boast one of the largest and most affluent populations of *mizrahim*, or Middle Eastern Jews. Item 4501 is a testament to this once vibrant center of Jewish culture. Following the rise of the Arab nationalist movement in the early twentieth century, many indigenous Jews were persecuted and eventually pushed out to neighboring Israel and elsewhere. The Jewish Agency for Israel estimates that there are no more than a dozen or so individual Jews who remain.

Case 4500 – Item Diagnostics

4501:	TORAH SCROLL
	Ink on parchment
	Baghdad, Iraq
	20th century
	GC.SCR.000199
4502:	HEBRON "GREAT DISASTER" LETTERS
	Ink on paper
	Hebron, Israel
	1834
	GC.PPR.010174, GC.PPR.010175, GC. PR.010176
4503:	RESCUED SCROLL
	Ink on parchment
	Uzbekistan
	19th century
	GC.SCR.001708

During the Ottoman period, Egyptian forces presided over many parts of what is modern Israel. In 1834, the Arabs of Hebron rebelled in an effort to gain autonomy. When the Jews of nearby Jerusalem appealed to Egyptian forces for protection, they received assurances that the Jewish Quarter would be spared. When the retaliation commenced, however, synagogues and homes throughout the quarter were looted while its inhabitants were subjected to horrific brutalities. These events were amplified in Hebron and Safed (northern Israel). Jewish-Arab aggressions became increasingly frequent following the British Mandate of Palestine at the end of WWI, and Israel's later state formation in 1948.

The event united Hebron's Sephardic and Ashkenasic communities, both of which had suffered greatly, and together they sent Rabbi Nathan Amram to Western Europe to seek aid. The letters displayed here recount these events and appeals to European allies (Item 4502). The two larger letters were written to Rabbi Amram by emissaries for the Egyptian government, one before and one after the pogrom. The smaller letter on green paper was written by Rabbi Amram himself, documenting his efforts to raise funds to replace Torahs desecrated during the incident. His signature can be seen at the bottom of the letter.

Anti-Semitism and acts of violence have been ongoing in Central Asia as well, particularly with the rise of Muslim extremism. In recent years, there have been synagogue burnings throughout the former Turko-Persian territories of the region. It is possible that Item 4503, from Uzbekistan, incurred its damage from one such event.

Anti-Semitism and the Pogroms of Europe   [Case 4600]

Through the Middle Ages and into the early modern era, hundreds of thousands of *ashkenazi*, or European Jews, were displaced. Many of these communities found sanctuary in Poland. Though not without turbulent periods of its own, the region had historically provided a political climate tolerant of ethnically diverse people groups and religions. This ethos is reflected in the Statute of Kalisz (1264) and the Warsaw Convention of the Polish-Lithuanian Commonwealth (1573), in which legal and religious rights were extended to Jewish citizenry. This state of coexistence would continue into the modern era, as demonstrated by Item 4601, one of many scrolls to have been produced in Lithuania during the seventeenth century. Vilna alone contained roughly 200 synagogues and prayer houses prior to WWII—when many would be desecrated and their sacred writings confiscated, like the scroll shown here.

Case 4600 – Item Diagnostics

4601:	BURNED TORAH SCROLL
	Ink on parchment
	Lithuania
	17th century
	GC.SCR.001912
4602:	BURNED TORAH SCROLL
	Ink on parchment
	Romania
	16th century
	GC.SCR.001929
4603:	BURNED TORAH SCROLL
	Ink on parchment
	Romania
	17th–18th century
	GC.SCR.001671

Elsewhere throughout Europe, persecutions continued. During the reign of Peter "the Lame," at the end of the sixteenth century, many Moldavian (and relatedly Romanian) Jews were expelled due to the much resented competition they created for local merchants. Items 4602 and 4603 attest to the remaining presence of a small Jewish community that would survive in Romania, up to the Socialist era when such objects were seized.

The safe haven that Poland provided eventually deteriorated with the partitioning of the Commonwealth at the end of the eighteenth century. Prussia, Russia, and the Habsburgs annexed these territories, retaining few of the liberties previously extended to local Jews. Following WWI, Poland returned briefly to the *paradisus Iudaeorum* ("Jewish Paradise") it had once been called. By the 1930s, just over three million Jews lived in Poland. With the ascendance of the Nazi regime, roughly 90% of this population would be exterminated.

The Holocaust and Kristallnacht

The Holocaust—known in Hebrew as *"HaShoah,"* or "The Catastrophe"—was the systematic persecution and murder of approximately six million Jews under the Nazi regime.

In the early morning hours of November 10, 1938, the first large-scale attack on Jews took place throughout Germany and Austria. The events of that night are remembered as *"Kristallnacht,"* or the "Night of Broken Glass."

On October 18, 1938, Adolf Hitler ordered over 12,000 Polish-born Jews to be deported from Germany to the Polish border. Unable to gain entry, they were forced to wait at the border station without food or money. When Herschel Grynszpan, a Jewish teenager living in Paris, heard that his family was among them, he responded with action. On November 7, Herschel went to the German Embassy in Paris and shot the Third Secretary, Ernst vom Rath, who died in the hospital two days later.

On the night of November 9, members of the Nazi assault division called *Sturmabteilung* (SA), the Nazi defense corps called *Schutzstaffel* (SS), or "Storm Detachment," and the Hitler Youth prepared a response to the shooting. Dressed in civilian clothes, they began 24 hours of violence in which approximately 91 Jews were killed. By the end of November 10, thousands of Jewish businesses were destroyed, over a thousand synagogues burned down, and more than 30,000 men between the ages of 16 and 60 arrested and transported to concentration camps or prison. This gallery offers a street-side glimpse of the destruction that took place on *Kristallnacht*.

Despite the inhumane acts committed against Jews, the Nazis believed that the Bible supported their actions. This room also looks at ways in which the Bible was used both to destroy and to protect Bible-related objects.

Hitler's Treatment of the Jews   [Case 4700]

While imprisoned in 1925 for a failed attempt to take over the German government, Adolf Hitler wrote a manifesto entitled *Mein Kampf* ("My Struggle"). In it, Hitler professed to recognize the legal rights credited to a religious institution. In the third chapter of *Mein Kampf*, Hitler writes, "To the political leader, the religious beliefs and institutions of his people must be sacred; otherwise, he has no right to be a politician." Elsewhere he goes on to say, "political parties should not meddle in religion." He never extended those rights to Judaism. This seems to be a clear contradiction in his philosophy and practice, but Hitler and the Nazis believed that Jews were merely a "parasitic race" who appeared to practice a religion in order to advance their global cause. So, in the minds of Nazi leaders, they were not infringing upon the rights of a religion by burning down synagogues, confiscating sacred scrolls (Item 4703), or desecrating Torah scrolls (Item 4704). According to Hitler, the Jews were not even German. They were diluting the quality of his "Aryan" race, and the question of their religious rights was irrelevant.

For Hitler, it was not enough for Jews to be removed from Germany. He believed that they should leave Germany with nothing. Nine days after *Kristallnacht*, on November 19, 1938, the Nazis established a devastating law for Jewish emigration: the Jews must pay a fine of 1 billion Reichsmarks, the currency of the Third Reich (Items 4701, 4702). If the fine was not paid by the Jewish community, they would be required to leave behind all their possessions before a single Jew was allowed to leave Germany. It was stated in the *Essener National Zeitung* that Germany "like the Pharaohs, will not permit any part of the Jewish possessions to leave the country." It was a crushing blow to many Jews, as most countries were not willing to bring in refugees without any assets.

Case 4700 – Item Diagnostics

4701:	COINS OF THE THIRD REICH Silver and various metals Germany 1938–1943 *On loan from a Private Collection*	4703:	JEREMIAH SCROLL AND BAG, DAMAGED DURING THE HOLOCAUST AND RECOVERED IN VILNA, LITHUANIA Ink on parchment and linen Poland or Ukraine 19th century GC.SCR.001923, GC.ARK.000880
4702:	1 RENTENMARK BILL, ORIGINALLY DESIGNED TO COMBAT HYPERINFLATION IN 1923 Paper Germany 1937 *On loan from a Private Collection*	4704:	WALLET MADE IN GERMANY FROM SECTIONS OF A TORAH SCROLL Ink on parchment Germany 1938–1945 GC.SCR.003681

The Sacred Torah Destroyed   [Case 4800]

There is no object within Judaism more sacred than the Torah. In Hebrew, Torah means "Law," but its importance runs much deeper than simply informing legal practices. It outlines the development of the Jewish people, from being freed from slavery in Egypt to being established in the land of Canaan. The Torah—comprised of the first five books of the Bible and attributed to Moses—has been transcribed from generation to generation. It is considered so sacred that Jews even avoid touching it. Because *"HaShem,"* or the "Divine Name," is written throughout the Torah, no observant Jew would ever think to let a Torah fall on the ground or be mishandled.

Case 4800 – Item Diagnostics

4801:	SONG OF SONGS SCROLL AND BAG, DAMAGED DURING THE HOLOCAUST AND RECOVERED IN VILNA, LITHUANIA Ink on parchment and linen Poland or Lithuania 19th century GC.SCR.001930, GC.ARK.000884
4802:	SAMUEL SCROLL AND BAG, DAMAGED DURING THE HOLOCAUST AND RECOVERED IN VILNA, LITHUANIA Ink on parchment and linen Eastern Europe 19th century GC.SCR.001919, GC.ARK.000876
4803:	TORAH SCROLL AND BAG **Recovered in Vilna, Lithuania** Ink on parchment and linen Poland Circa 1900 GC.SCR.001918, GC.ARK.000875

It is with this knowledge that Jews across Hitler's Reich witnessed the horrible mistreatment of Torah scrolls during *Kristallnacht* and throughout the Holocaust. Torah scrolls were thrown out windows and unrolled on the streets for Hitler Youth to dance on and ride bikes over. Scrolls were piled up with furniture and burned in the streets as the synagogue from which they came was also engulfed in flames. Firefighters were seen standing by to ensure the fires did not spread to any non-Jewish buildings while policemen looked on to make sure the German "civilians" (the SS, SA, or Hitler Youth in civilian clothes) weren't disrupted. In Vienna, some SA members even went as far as forcing a Rabbi to throw a Torah into the Danube River.

Some scrolls were confiscated and catalogued instead of being destroyed. One such occurrence took place in Vilna, Lithuania, known to Jews as "the Jerusalem of the North." The Nazi's recovered a large number of Torah scrolls and placed them in the State Library (Items 4801, 4802, 4803).

The "Man of the Year" and Those Who Stood against Him   [Case 4900]

In May of 1919, after Germany lost the First World War, the Allies presented the full terms of peace to Germany in the Hall of Mirrors at Versailles, France. Germany had to return territory in France, Denmark, and Belgium, plus all of its colonies in Asia and Africa. The treaty also called for Germany to pay enormous reparations that would cripple the country for years, causing the mark to plummet in value (4 billion marks was equal to one dollar by 1923). Germany also needed to dissolve its military, retaining an army of only 100,000, a nearly suicidal requirement considering Russia's ominous presence.

Adolf Hitler blatantly overturned every portion of this treaty after he seized power as chancellor of Germany on January 30, 1933. Over the next six to seven years, Hitler systematically reversed the Treaty of Versailles by restoring territories back to Germany (often through quiet but brutal force) and building up Germany's military. Hitler's popularity soared. Many Germans were unable to recognize the evil among them because Hitler was emphatically removing the shame of the First World War and its final treaty. In many minds, Hitler was the savior of Germany.

On January 2, 1939, *Time* magazine singled out Adolf Hitler as 1938's "Man of the Year" (Item 4901). *Time's* "Man of the Year" is selected based on significance and not necessarily quality of character, a balance demonstrated by the selection of Hitler and the cover's horrific lithograph. A month before publication, Ralph Ingersoll (a publisher at *Time*) discovered this lithograph that captured the atrocity of stories that were beginning to come out of Germany concerning the mistreatment of Jews and other "undesirables."

The Nazis sought to label these "undesirables" so they could be seen and categorized on sight. By command of the SS General Reinhard Heydrich, Jews across Hitler's Reich were forced to wear identification badges in the shape of the six-pointed Jewish "Star of David." (Items 4903, 4904).

Some Germans recognized the corruption that had beset their beloved country, and risked their lives to undermine their inhumane government. One was Lutheran pastor Dietrich Bonhoeffer. Bonhoeffer was involved in one of the plots to assassinate Hitler. He joined the *Abwehr* (a German intelligence organization similar to the CIA or FBI) as a sort of "double-agent," and participated in safely smuggling seven Jews out of Germany in *Operation 7*. In 1940, Bonhoeffer also publicly declared his defiance by publishing a book on the Psalms titled *The Prayer Book of the Bible*, which emphasized the Old Testament's importance by implication and used pro-Jewish language throughout (Item 4902). Considering the political climate in Germany at the time, this publication was nothing short of explosive. The Nazis forbade Bonhoeffer from publishing another word.

Case 4900 – Item Diagnostics

4901:	TIME MAGAZINE, 1938 "MAN OF THE YEAR" EDITION: ADOLF HITLER Ink on paper New York City, New York January 2, 1939 GC.PAM.000277	4903:	UNUSED STAR OF DAVID BADGE WITH THE INSCRIPTION "JUDE" (GERMAN FOR "JEW") Linen Germany 1945 GC.FIC.000019
4902:	DIETRICH BONHOEFFER, THE PRAYER BOOK OF THE BIBLE *"If we are persecuted for the sake of the cause of God, then we suffer innocently, and we suffer with God himself…"* Ink on paper Bad Salzuflen, Germany 1953 GC.PAM.000276	4904:	STAR OF DAVID BADGE WITH THE INSCRIPTION "JOOD" (DUTCH FOR "JEW") Linen The Netherlands 1944 GC.OBJ.000165

Building on a History of Anti-Semitism   [Case 5000]

Hitler was not the first person to advocate violent anti-Semitism. Hatred of the Jewish people had been practiced in Europe for centuries. Even Martin Luther, in his old age and amid numerous health problems, turned bitterly anti-Semitic. In his 1543 work, *On the Jews and Their Lies*, Luther went so far as to suggest that Jewish synagogues "should be set on fire, and whatever does not burn up should be covered or spread over with dirt." When the Nazis did just that, they saw themselves as taking the words of a national icon and putting them into action. Hitler adopted the language of historical anti-Semitism, using the Jews as the scapegoat for Germany's troubles. According to Hitler, Germany's defeat in the First World War and its current economic woes were results of "the Jewish problem." Blinded by his hatred of Jews, Hitler chose to ignore the fact that 12,000 patriotic Germans of Jewish ethnicity died in the First World War fighting for their country.

Despite the holes in the Nazi argument, anti-Semitic conclusions were made and evidence was created to support those conclusions. On *Kristallnacht*, Jewish synagogues were burned by the dozens, and Hitler Youth were seen tossing Torah scrolls into brooks and tearing them up in the streets (Item 5003). Sacred Torah scrolls, formerly treated by Jews with the utmost reverence, were cut up and used as if they were regular pieces of leather to make a wide variety of items (Item 5002). Then, on November 12, the Nazis announced that the Jews would have to pay for all the damage done to Jewish property. The acts of *Kristallnacht* had launched the Jews headlong into the darkest years of the Holocaust.

On November 15, the SS newspaper *Das Schwarze Korps* ("The Black Corps") violently alluded to what was to come, citing the language of the Hebrew Bible:

> "We shall use our Jewish hostages in a systematic way, no matter how shocking some people find it. We shall use the principle proclaimed by the Jews—'an eye for an eye and a tooth for a tooth.' But we shall take a thousand eyes for one eye, a thousand teeth for one tooth."

Case 5000 – Item Diagnostics

5001:	TORAH SCROLL AND BAG, DAMAGED DURING THE HOLOCAUST AND RECOVERED IN VILNA, LITHUANIA Ink on parchment and linen Poland 19th century GC.SCR.001913, GC.ARK.000870	5003:	TORAH SCROLL DAMAGED DURING THE HOLOCAUST, KNIFE CUTS AND HOLES THROUGHOUT THE SCROLL Ink on parchment Germany Mid-19th century GC.SCR.003430
5002:	SATCHEL MADE DURING THE HOLOCAUST FROM SECTIONS OF A TORAH SCROLL Ink on parchment Eastern Europe 1938–1945 GC.SCR.002054	5004:	PARTIAL TORAH SCROLL AND BAG **Damaged during the Holocaust and Recovered in Vilna, Lithuania** Ink on parchment and linen Eastern Europe 18th century GC.SCR.001922, GC.ARK.000879

Vilna: The Jerusalem of the North   [Case 5100]

By the 1930s, the city of Vilna—located in modern Lithuania—had been the object of diplomatic debate for some time. Both Lithuania and Poland claimed the city after the First World War, but as the Second World War approached, Vilna was officially absorbed by Poland. In September 1939, Soviet forces occupied Vilna and other parts of eastern Poland in accordance with the German-Soviet Pact. Less than two years later, Germany attacked Eastern Europe, claiming Vilna from the Soviets on June 24, 1941.

In the period between the World Wars, Vilna had a Jewish population of over 50,000. The city had dozens of synagogues and was an important center for the *yeshivot*, institutions focused entirely on organized study of the Torah and other books of the Hebrew Bible. These Jews faced immediate oppression under Nazi occupation. Within the first two months after taking Vilna, the Nazis killed nearly 9,000 Jews in the Ponary forest, just outside the city. Jews elsewhere in Lithuania were being relocated to the ghettos and labor camps around Vilna. By the end of the year, around 40,000 Jews were murdered in the Ponary massacre.

On November 27, 1941, the Jews of the Vilna ghetto were ordered to declare all cultural objects in the ghetto—

including Judaica (Jewish religious items)—and deposit them in the State Library. While some of the objects were used to record a history of the ghetto, many more objects were prepared to be sent away for scholarly study or to be put to other purposes. At the end of the war, a large number of Jewish scrolls were found in the Vilna library and recovered (Items 5101, 5102).

Case 5100 – Item Diagnostics

5101:	PARTIAL TORAH SCROLL, RESCUED FROM THE HOLOCAUST Contains Genesis through the giving of "The Law" in Exodus, concluding with a post-Holocaust dedication: *"Torah sheets plucked from the fire from the Germans…"* Ink on parchment Germany 19th century GC.SCR.000486	5102:	TORAH SCROLL AND BAG, DAMAGED DURING THE HOLOCAUST AND RECOVERED IN VILNA, LITHUANIA Ink on parchment and linen Eastern Europe 18th century GC.SCR.001921, GC.ARK.000878

The Bible and the Holocaust   [Case 5200]

Poland and its Jewish population suffered some of the most brutal atrocities of the Holocaust. Concentration camps and death camps like Aushwitz, Sobibor, and Majdanek were all located in Poland. As the Nazi wave of destruction tore through Europe, many synagogues and Torah scrolls in Poland were destroyed or suffered fire damage (Item 5201). Though Hitler encouraged the destruction of Jewish Torahs, he himself refers to the Law of Moses numerous times in *Mein Kampf*. For example, in an argument on racial purity, Hitler paraphrases Deuteronomy 23:2 by saying, "The sins of the fathers will be visited on the tenth generation."

Case 5200 – Item Diagnostics

5201:	TORAH SCROLL WITH SMOKE, FIRE, AND WATER DAMAGE Ink on parchment Germany 17th–18th century GC.SCR.001641

The Bible, however, was also cited by many people who were working to help the Jews. The Barmen Declaration authored in May 1934 by Karl Barth and others, denounced the anti-Semitism coming from the "German Christians" (the most popular Christian denomination in the Third Reich). At one point, it reads:

If you find that we are speaking contrary to Scripture [the Bible], then do not listen to us! But if you find that we are taking our stand upon Scripture, then let no fear or temptation keep you from treading with us the path of faith and obedience to the Word of God…

The entire declaration was published in the London Times on June 4, 1934.

Defacing Sacred Texts   [Case 5300]

The Nazis desecrated Torah scrolls in many ways. Some Torah scrolls went through a form of desecration where they were cut to pieces and used for countless purposes. Strips of parchment from Torah scrolls were used to line and reinforce bags, book covers, and even musical instruments like a drum. The parchment would be sewn together to make table runners (Item 5301) or to line the inside of shoes (Item 5302). To the Nazis, the material on which the Torah was written was more valuable than the words it contained.

Case 5300 – Item Diagnostics

5301:	WALL COVERING OR TABLE RUNNER MADE FROM SECTIONS OF A TORAH SCROLL Ink on parchment Eastern Europe 19th and 20th century GC.SCR.001464	5302:	SHOE INSERTS MADE FROM A TORAH SCROLL Ink on parchment Eastern Europe 18th and 20th century GC.SCR.002052.1-.2

Movement 3—Translation

For more than two thousand years, translation has been an important part of the Bible's history. This section examines how the process of translation has made the Bible accessible to many different cultures while still remaining true to the original text.

Around the second or third century BC, Jewish scholars collaborated to produce the Septuagint, a Greek translation of the Hebrew Bible. With the spread of Christianity, translation became more common. By the year AD 1000, large portions of the Christian Bible had been translated into dozens of languages. As new resources became available, scholars were able to produce more accurate translations of the biblical text for more people. Today, various organizations continue to produce translations of the Bible in new languages.

Historically, translators have faced numerous difficulties in their work. In some cases they were translating for people with no formal system of written language. In others their very lives have been in danger.

Jerome's Cave

In the late fourth century AD, St. Jerome lived in the caves of Bethlehem, working on a new translation of the Bible into Latin from the original Greek and Hebrew. His work, now known as the Vulgate (from the Latin word for "common") was commissioned by Pope Damasus I. As early as the third century AD, a group of translations collectively known as the "Old Latin" version was available throughout Europe and North Africa, but it was imperfect in many respects. Jerome's Vulgate standardized the Latin text and corrected many of the errors and inconsistencies of the earlier text.

In order to improve his understanding of the Hebrew language and Jewish biblical commentary, Jerome moved to Bethlehem, where he spent the last years of his life. Jerome was a prolific writer, and a number of his personal letters circulated during the Middle Ages. In a letter to his friend Pammachius, he explained the difficulties of translation, saying,

> "For I myself not only admit but freely proclaim that in translating from the Greek (except in the case of the holy scriptures where even the order of the words is a mystery) I render sense for sense and not word for word… [Yet,] in dealing with the scriptures it is the sense we have to look to and not the words."

Jerome's translation eventually became the standard Bible translation of Medieval Europe; however, it took several centuries before it gained widespread acceptance.

In this gallery, you can ask Jerome questions about his life and works. There is also a table with ink and quills, where you can experience how difficult it is to copy texts by hand!

Early Translations of the Bible

The history of biblical translation begins with the Jewish Bible. According to an ancient text called the *Letter of Aristeas*, written in the Hellenistic period, roughly seventy Jewish scholars collaborated to translate the Hebrew Law into Greek. This version, called the Septuagint ("LXX"), enabled Greek-speaking Jews to read the biblical text.

At the beginning of the first century AD came the birth of a new religion: Christianity. One of the central tenets of Christianity is the charge to share the gospel (which means "the good news") about Jesus with the whole world. As Christianity spread, people began to translate its sacred text—the Bible—into new languages. By AD 500, translations of portions of the Bible existed in more than half a dozen languages, including Coptic, Aramaic, Latin, Gothic (or Old German), Georgian, and Ge'ez. These translation efforts tended to focus on the sections of the Bible that were most central to Christian worship and liturgical practices—namely, the Gospels and the Psalms—though many other parts of the Bible were also translated.

Greek Septuagint: The Earliest Written Bible Translations   [Case 5400]
The oldest books of the Bible were composed in Hebrew, the language of ancient Israel. Portions of Ezra and Daniel were written in Aramaic, a Semitic language closely related to Hebrew.

In 336-323 BC, the conquests of Alexander the Great spread Greek culture and language throughout much of the Mediterranean world and inaugurated the Hellenistic period. Over the next two or three centuries, Jewish communities gradually translated their sacred texts from Hebrew and Aramaic into Greek.

Case 5400 – Item Diagnostics

5401:	GENESIS 29 IN GREEK, SCROLL FRAGMENT ON RE-USED PAPYRUS Ink on papyrus Egypt Circa late 2nd century AD GC.PAP.000389
5402:	PSALMS 112-114 (CXI-CXIII) IN GREEK, CODEX FRAGMENT FROM P. BODMER XXIV Ink on papyrus Egypt 3rd–4th century AD GC.MS.000170.46
5403:	1 SAMUEL 23 IN GREEK, CODEX FRAGMENT FROM P. FEINBERG 1 Ink on papyrus Egypt 4th century AD GC.PAP.000504.1

The earliest translations were likely produced in Egypt. They began in the third century BC with the books of the Torah, Genesis through Deuteronomy (Item 5401). According to the *Letter of Aristeas*, an ancient Jewish text written sometime before the late first century AD, this project was commissioned by Ptolemy Philadelphus, king of Egypt (285-247 BC). At Ptolemy's request, the high priest in Jerusalem selected seventy-two elders—six from each of the twelve tribes of Israel—to translate the Jewish Law (Torah) into Greek for the king's library. This legend is the origin of the term "Septuagint," meaning "seventy." Written in Roman numerals as "LXX," this term serves as an abbreviation for the number of translators reported in the legend.

Modern scholars think that different communities or individuals initially translated the different books of the Hebrew Bible. At the time, there was no "Bible" yet, but collections of multiple scrolls. We do not know exactly where, when, or why each scroll was first translated. In some books, including Psalms and 1 Samuel, the Greek follows the Hebrew original rather literally (Items 5402, 5403). In other books, such as Isaiah, Proverbs, Esther, Job, and Daniel, the translation is more "free," rendering thought-for-thought rather than word-for-word. Such contrasts suggest that the earliest translations were not unified by a single plan. The common denominator is that all were produced by Jewish translators prior to the birth of Christianity.

In its oldest sense, the label "Septuagint" (LXX) applies only to the books of Genesis through Deuteronomy. In subsequent centuries, its usage widened to include Greek translations of all the other books as well. Since the third century AD, scholars have used this title to distinguish the earliest translations of each book, or the "Old Greek," from much later attempts to re-translate the Hebrew Bible into Greek.

Each of the Greek fragments exhibited here has a complex history. First, since they represent three different books, they likely originated from three distinct Jewish translation projects. Second, by the time these manuscripts were copied four to six centuries later, the earliest translations had undergone various revisions. One task for scholars who study fragments of this sort is to figure out the history of revision.

Jerome's Latin Vulgate [Case 5500]

Translations of the Bible into Latin probably began to spring up along the outskirts of the Roman Empire within a century of the New Testament's composition, particularly in North Africa and Gaul on the northwestern edge of Europe. Fewer people in these regions would have been familiar with Greek, so the biblical text needed to be in a language they understood. These older translations into Latin were never uniform, but were known collectively as the "Old Latin Version" of the Bible.

Case 5500 – Item Diagnostics

5501:	**ST. JEROME,** *LETTERS AND AGAINST VIGILANTIUS*
	Decorated manuscript on parchment
	Northern Italy
	Circa 1450–1485
	GC.MS.000453
5502:	**PSALTER OF ST. ROMUALD**
	PSALMS 99:3-4 AND 100:1-8
	Ink on parchment
	Camaldoli, Italy
	Mid-9th century AD
	GC.MS.000569
5503:	**HATTEM VULGATE**
	Illuminated manuscript on parchment
	Hattem, Netherlands
	Circa 1420–1430
	GC.MS.00159

In the late fourth century AD, St. Jerome saw the need for a new Latin translation, now known as the Latin Vulgate, to correct the errors of the Old Latin translations. His *Letters* (Item 5501) paint a detailed picture of his thoughts during this period, including discussions of the best methods of translation.

Though it took several centuries to gain acceptance, the Vulgate eventually became the standard Bible translation throughout Europe for more than a thousand years, being read by everyone from ninth-century saints (Item 5502) to members of a fifteenth-century movement called the *Devotio Moderna* (Item 5503). One reason why Jerome's translation finally achieved prominence across Europe was that his translation of the Bible was the version used in the liturgy. Few people in the Middle Ages were able to read, so most people primarily encountered the Bible when it was read at church. Therefore, as Christian liturgy spread from Rome through the church's missionary efforts, Jerome's translation also spread across the continent.

Early Vernacular Translation in Northeastern Africa and Palestine   [Case 5600]

The Greek and Latin translations shown earlier in this gallery made Jewish and Christian scriptures available in languages that were widely used throughout the Hellenistic and Roman empires. In many communities, however, Greek and Latin served as second languages rather than the mother tongue.

The early translations exhibited in this case served more regionally specific needs. They made the texts of the Christian Bible available in languages native to Egypt (Items 5601, 5602), Palestine (Item 5603), and Ethiopia (Item 5604).

Coptic was the latest stage in the Egyptian language. In the third century AD, around the time that Coptic Bible translations first arose, the spoken language had been used for over two millennia, but Greek had eclipsed Egyptian writing. Coptic employed a new writing system that used the Greek alphabet plus a few letters from the native Demotic script for sounds not adequately represented in Greek. Coptic flourished for many centuries in multiple local dialects, including Sahidic.

Different books of the Bible were initially translated into Coptic under diverse circumstances, rather than as a one-time project. The two examples shown here were both based on Greek manuscripts, but with one important distinction. New Testament books were written in Greek, so this Sahidic Coptic version of Ephesians was translated directly from the original language of composition (Item 5602). By contrast, Old Testament books were composed in Hebrew. In relying on a Greek version, this Coptic fragment of Psalms is thus a translation of a translation (Item 5601).

The Gospels were translated into Aramaic sometime between the fourth and sixth centuries AD. These translations were based on Greek, the original language of the Gospels. But the Gospels themselves were translating words that had been originally spoken in Aramaic (attested most famously in Matthew 27:46 by Jesus' quotation of Psalm 22 from the cross: "Eli, Eli, lema sabachthani?"). The translation shown in the brown ink on this palimpsest (Item 5603) thus creates an interesting linguistic circle, as it re-presents the words of Jesus in a dialect very close to the one that he would have used. The translation is written in a cursive Syriac script known as Estrangela.

Like Hebrew, Ge'ez is a Semitic language. No manuscripts from the early history of Bible translations into Ge'ez have survived, but inscriptions from the sixth century show that at least the Psalms were translated by then. Surviving manuscripts suggest that the Psalms and the Gospels (Item 5604) were the biblical books used most extensively.

Both Sahidic Coptic and Ge'ez are still used as official languages of worship by congregations in Egypt and Ethiopia today.

Case 5600 – Item Diagnostics

5601:	PSALMS 111-112 (CX-CXI) IN SAHIDIC COPTIC, CODEX FRAGMENT Ink on parchment Egypt 6th–7th century AD GC.MS.000503.2	5603:	LEAF FROM THE CODEX CLIMACI RESCRIPTUS, GOSPELS MANUSCRIPT IN CHRISTIAN PALESTINIAN ARAMAIC, REUSED FOR "THE LADDER OF DIVINE ASCENT" IN SYRIAC Ink on parchment Sinai, Egypt Circa 6th century AD and 9th century AD GC.MS.000149.66
5602:	EPHESIANS 4-5 IN SAHIDIC COPTIC, BIFOLIUM FRAGMENT Ink on papyrus Egypt 4th century AD GC.PAP.000414	5604:	GOSPEL OF JOHN, IN GE'EZ, WITH CARRYING CASE Decorated manuscript on parchment Ethiopia Mid- to late 18th century GC.MS.000124.1-.2

Medieval European Translations and Conversation in a Peasants' Village (Video)

During the Middle Ages, Latin ceased to be a first language for people in Europe. Instead, Europeans were speaking early forms of modern languages like French, German, and English. Latin was still a common language, since it was the language of education and the Church, but it was no longer the language of "commoners." As such, people around Europe began to push for translations of the Bible into the vernacular, or commonly spoken, languages of the day. Church officials often met these translation movements with opposition and, sometimes, persecution.

These galleries present the story of medieval Bible translation into the vernacular. As you enter the peasants' village, you will pass between two small houses where a couple of hard-working women are talking together through their windows. When their discussion turns to religion, the women disagree about whether or not to be excited about the new, unapproved translation of the Bible into English. Here you will also see a number of manuscripts and early printed copies of the Bible, newly translated into some of the vernacular languages of medieval Europe.

Bible Translation in Continental Europe   [Case 5700]

Case 5700 – Item Diagnostics

5701:	LECTIONARY, IN DUTCH
	Translation by Johannes Scutkin
	Ink on paper
	Circa 1480
	GC.MS.000337
5702:	BOOK OF PSALMS FROM A BIBLE, IN FRENCH
	Illuminated manuscript on parchment
	France
	14th century
	GC.MS.000136
5703:	*VOLKSBIBEL*, IN GERMAN, VOLUME V, FACSIMILE
	Illuminated manuscript
	Graz, Austria
	Circa 1467
	GC.PBK.000381.5

The three items in this case reflect some of the vernacular Bible translations that were beginning to appear on the European continent in the late Middle Ages. Translations of certain books of the Bible into French began appearing during the twelfth century, with the first full translations appearing in the mid-thirteenth century. Item 5701 is the book of Psalms from a larger illuminated Bible, probably commissioned by a wealthy French patron. Other Bible translations, such as Johannes Scutkin's northern Dutch translation (Item 5702), grew out of movements like the Brothers and Sisters of the Common Life. In Germany, manuscript Bibles like the *Volksbibel* (Item 5703) relied on vernacular translation and illumination to communicate the stories of the Bible to the uneducated population.

Old Church Slavonic: A Literary Language for the Slavs   [Case 5800]

In the ninth century, a pair of brothers, St. Cyril and St. Methodius, traveled as Christian missionaries to Great Moravia (Slovakia and the Czech Republic) from Thessalonica, Greece. One of their main tasks was to standardize the first Slavic literary language so that it could be used for translating the Bible. This language has come to be known as Old Church Slavonic, and it is an older version of the liturgical language still used by the Russian Orthodox Church. As part of the preparation for their mission, Cyril and Methodius set about translating some of the most frequently used portions of the Bible, including the Psalter, the Book of Acts, and Gospel lectionaries (Item 3701).

Case 5800 – Item Diagnostics

5801:	GOSPEL LECTIONARY, IN OLD CHURCH SLAVONIC
	Illuminated manuscript on parchment
	Russia
	Circa 1550–1560
	GC.MS.000276

This *Aprakos*, or Gospel Lectionary, is not arranged according to the regular order of Gospel passages as found in the New Testament, but rather according to the order in which they would be read throughout the church year. When Cyril and Methodius were translating "the gospels" for their mission, they were likely translating from a Byzantine copy of a Greek lectionary. In fact, it is possible that a copy of the Gospels, arranged from beginning to end, did not exist in Old Church Slavonic until some centuries after their original mission.

The different sections open with decorative banded headpieces in the Balkan Style, incorporating a complex interlacing of white bands popular in the fifteenth and sixteenth centuries. It also contains four full-page portraits of the Evangelists, and is open to the portrait of Saint John.

Bible in Old and Middle English   [Case 5900]

It is said that around AD 735, the Venerable Bede produced a translation of the Gospel of John into Old English, though that work has not survived. Manuscript copies of partial Bible translation into various Old English dialects have come down to us from the ninth and tenth centuries, indicating that vernacular translation was an acceptable practice in Anglo-Saxon England, if not common. Later, printed editions of these early manuscripts were produced to provide historical support for Bible translation into the vernacular in the newly founded Church of England (Item 5903).

Case 5900 – Item Diagnostics

5901:	THE GOSPELS IN ANGLO-SAXON, FIRST EDITION
	Printed by John Daye
	Ink on paper
	London, England
	1571
	GC.BIB.001281
5902:	THE ROSEBERY ROLLE, OR THE PSALMS AND CANTICLES IN PRE-WYCLIFFITE ENGLISH TRANSLATION, WITH COMMENTARY BY RICHARD ROLLE
	Decorated manuscript on paper
	Yorkshire, England
	Late 14th to early 15th century
	GC.MS.000148
5903:	JOHN PURVEY, PROLOGUE TO THE WYCLIFFE BIBLE
	Printed by Robert Crowley
	Ink on paper
	London, England
	1550
	GC.PBK.000828

For several centuries after the Norman conquest of England, the English language was no longer used in manuscripts. Middle English, a blend of Old English and Norman French, began to be written down in the fourteenth century. Richard Rolle, an English hermit living in Yorkshire, England, wrote a commentary on the Psalms and Canticles (other songs found throughout the Bible), which included their full English translations. He compiled the commentary for a local nun, Margaret Kirkby, so that she could understand what she recited in her cell. The manuscript on display here—known as the Rosebery Rolle—is one of the two earliest known copies of Rolle's work, and was likely copied for a convent of nuns in Rolle's native Yorkshire (Item 5901).

Later in the fourteenth century, John Wycliffe, a scholar at the University of Oxford, and his followers—known as "Wycliffites" or "Lollards"—advocated a number of reforms to the social and ecclesiastical order of their day. In the 1380s, the Lollards produced a translation of the Bible from Latin into Middle English. Though it is uncertain whether Wycliffe was directly involved with the project, this new translation came to bear his name. For this, Wycliffe is often seen as a precursor to the Reformation. One of Wycliffe's followers, John Purvey, wrote a prologue to the Wycliffite Bible translation, in which he addresses the translation project, the translators' desire to make the Bible available in the vernacular, and the importance of reading the Bible (Item 5902).

Non-European Translations of the Bible

During the Middle Ages, important vernacular translations of the Bible were also being produced in the Middle East. Unlike their predominantly Christian counterparts in Europe, both Jews and Christians initiated translation projects in the Middle East. Jewish translations of the Tanakh often accompanied lengthy scriptural commentaries by prominent Jewish teachers like Maimonides, Judah Halevi, and Saadia Gaon. It is possible that their translations were also intended as a form of commentary, making clear the meanings of the sacred truths contained in the original Hebrew. Translations of the Christian Bible into Syriac, Armenian, and Arabic were also produced. This gallery arranges some of the more significant Jewish and Christian translations according to linguistic or regional groupings.

The Tanakh in Aramaic and Samaritan   [Case 6000]

During the Middle Ages, Jewish vernacular translations were increasingly important. Judeo-Aramaic is a Semitic language greatly influenced by Hebrew. It was one of the most common vernacular languages in the Middle East from the sixth century BC well into the Jewish diaspora. A translation of and commentary upon the Tanakh into Aramaic is known as a *targum* (plural, *targumim*). It developed when Hebrew was becoming less common as a spoken language, and was used only for education and worship. Though writing the *targumim* down was prohibited, there is evidence of such activity as early as the first century BC. The two most famous *targumim* are the *Targum Onkelos* on the Torah and the *Targum Jonathan ben Uzziel* on the prophets (Item 6002). These are still used as liturgical texts by Jews in Yemen.

Case 6000 – Item Diagnostics

6001:	SAMARITAN PENTATEUCH, IN SAMARITAN HEBREW SCRIPT
	Ink on parchment
	Israel
	12th–13th century
	GC.MS.000358
6002:	BOOK OF PROPHETS, IN HEBREW AND ARAMAIC
	Ink on parchment
	Yemen
	15th century
	GC.MS.000473

Another important version in the history of the Tanakh is the Samaritan Pentateuch. The Samaritan alphabet derives from the Paleo-Hebrew alphabet, drawing from ancient forms of the standard Hebrew letters and hardly resembling the standard, "square" Hebrew alphabet at all. Samaritans have their own version of the Pentateuch (Item 6001), which is written in Samaritan Hebrew script and contains over 6,000 differences from the standard Masoretic text. Almost one-third of these differences agree with the Greek Septuagint.

Bible Manuscripts in Syriac and Armenian   [Case 6100]

The Syriac language belongs to an Aramaic group of languages, and was spoken in the first millennium AD throughout much of the region between Israel and Iraq. The earliest Syriac translation of the New Testament—called the *Peshitta*—was prepared between the first and second centuries AD, and is most likely the earliest translation of the New Testament from the original Greek. Like the Vulgate and other early Bible translations, the text of the *Peshitta* has remained constant since its creation and continues to be used as a liturgical language. Over the centuries, the *Peshitta* was widely used among the Christians of the Middle East, and is still being used today by the Syriac Orthodox Church.

There are two *Peshittas* in this case. The first dates from the ninth century AD (Item 6101). Though the text is extremely faded, this manuscript is remarkable in that it still features a very early (perhaps original) decorative

Case 6100 – Item Diagnostics

6101:	PESHITTA, IN SYRIAC
	Ink on parchment, with wooden cover boards
	Iraq
	9th century AD
	GC.MS.000228
6102:	KHABOURIS CODEX, IN SYRIAC
	Ink on parchment
	Iraq
	11th century AD
	GC.MS.000283
6103:	GOSPEL BOOK, IN ARMENIAN, WITH ILLUMINATIONS BY THE ARTIST GHAZAR
	Illuminated manuscript on parchment
	Cilicia, Province of Ekeghiats
	Circa 1100–1400
	GC.MS.000274.2

wooden binding. The second is the Khabouris Codex (Item 6102). The Khabouris Codex is a complete *Peshitta*, or traditional Syriac New Testament, minus some disputed books: 2 Peter, 2 John, 3 John, Jude and the Book of Revelation. Though this manuscript dates to the eleventh century, a scribal note records that this codex was copied from a much older *Peshitta*, dating to the second century AD.

Armenian is an Indo-European language, sharing similarities with Latin, Greek, and English. Christian theologian Mesrop Mashtots (d. AD 440) developed the Armenian alphabet in the fifth century AD. The earliest examples of literary Armenian that we have are translations of the Bible, also from the fifth century. The Armenian Gospel Book on display (Item 6103) was written and illuminated in the fifteenth century AD by the artist Ghazar, but contains leaves from an older, twelfth-century manuscript, which was commissioned by "the Crown Prince Kostandin, the King's Chamberlain." These twelfth-century leaves feature beautifully illuminated headbands at the opening of each Gospel, as can be seen here.

Judeo-Arabic and Arabic Translations [Case 6200]

Judeo-Arabic is a form of Arabic that is written using the Hebrew alphabet and spoken by Middle Eastern Jews, beginning in the Middle Ages. Many important Jewish theologians wrote in Judeo-Arabic, including Maimonides, Judah Halevi, and the Saadia Gaon, who is widely considered the founder of Judeo-Arabic literature. In addition to the many grammatical, linguistic, and philosophical texts he wrote, the Saadia Gaon also produced translations of the Tanakh into Judeo-Arabic, accompanied by his own exegesis. Other commentators followed suit (Items 6201, 6202).

Christian translations of the Bible have also been made into Arabic, often for liturgical purposes (Item 6203).

Case 6200 – Item Diagnostics

6201:	PSALMS WITH COMMENTARY BY TANHUM BEN YOSEF, IN JUDEO-ARABIC	6203:	LITURGICAL MANUSCRIPT, IN ARABIC
	Ink on paper		Ink on paper
	Egypt		Egypt
	13th century		13th century
	GC.MS.000470		GC.MS.000227
6202:	PENTATEUCH, IN ARABIZED JUDEO-ARABIC HEBREW, ARAMAIC, AND ARABIC		
	Ink on parchment		
	Andalusia		
	14th–15th century		
	GC.MS.000457		

The Contribution of William Tyndale

This gallery has two rooms. One recreates the scene of William Tyndale's 1536 execution, as illustrated in John Foxe's famous book *The Acts and Monuments*, more commonly known as *Foxe's Book of Martyrs*. Tyndale had been illegally printing portions of his English translation of the New Testament on the European continent and smuggling them into England and Scotland. He was eventually caught, tried as a heretic, found guilty, and condemned to death. Rather than being burned alive, he was sentenced to death by strangulation, a courtesy given to educated men like Tyndale. His body was burned immediately after his death.

You can hear the executioner telling Tyndale to speak his last words, to make his peace with God, and to get on with it quickly. Tyndale responds with an explanation of his actions. His final plea is, "Lord, open the king of England's eyes." Two years later, King Henry VIII of England legalized the first "authorized" English Bible—the Great Bible—which was published in 1539 and based on Tyndale's New Testament translation.

In another room, you find important theological writings by Tyndale and early versions of his translations. Prior to his death, Tyndale finished translating the New Testament, the Pentateuch, and the book of Jonah. It is also thought that he completed English translations of Joshua through 2 Chronicles, though they only appeared after his death in the printing of the Matthew's Bible (a Bible completed by Tyndale's apprentice John Rogers). These translations were important to later English versions of the Bible.

William Tyndale and Early English Reform   [Case 6300]

Case 6300 – Item Diagnostics

6301:	**WILLIAM TYNDALE,** *OBEDIENCE OF A CHRISTIAN MAN*
	Printed by Merten de Keyser
	Ink on paper
	Antwerp, Belgium
	1528
	GC.PBK.000367
6302:	**WILLIAM TYNDALE,** *PRACTICE OF PRELATES*
	Printed by Merten de Keyser
	Ink on paper
	Antwerp, Belgium
	1530
	GC.PBK.000678

William Tyndale (ca. 1494–1536) was a writer of theology and a translator of the Bible. He is known for his English translation of the Bible, but also for his views on the Church of England, Protestant reform, and theological interpretations of scripture. In his *Practice of Prelates* (Item 6302), Tyndale criticizes the English church and King Henry VIII's excuse for his divorce from Catherine of Aragon. Tyndale places the blame directly on the English Cardinal Thomas Wolsey. His text not only condemns the King's divorce, it also rejects the legitimacy of his second marriage to Anne Boleyn. Ironically, Tyndale's earlier work, *Obedience of a Christian Man* (Item 6301), was read by Henry and is believed to have influenced his decision to break from the Roman Catholic Church. Henry declared himself the head of the Church of England, forever removing papal authority. *Obedience of a Christian Man* is one of Tyndale's most important works, addressing major issues of the English Reformation. In it, Tyndale rejects the allegorical interpretation of the Bible, arguing that it results in theological error.

Translations, Dissent, and Execution   [Case 6400]

Earlier reformers like Martin Luther influenced William Tyndale. After his time studying theology at Oxford and Cambridge, Tyndale went to London in 1523 to seek patronage for an English translation of the Bible. He was quickly identified as being a dissenter and was eventually forced to flee England. He began translating the

Bible into English using as many of the Hebrew and Greek manuscripts as possible, for he was skilled in Hebrew, Greek, Latin, German, Spanish, Italian, and French. The first edition of Tyndale's New Testament was printed, in part, in 1525 (Item 6401). The work began in Cologne, but was interrupted when Tyndale was forced to flee to Worms, resulting in the first full edition being released in 1526 (Item 6402). These early editions are rare, as the English clergy burned many in disapproval. In 1535, Tyndale was captured and imprisoned for heresy, but this did not stop his efforts of translation and revision. The 1535 fragment seen in this case is the sole surviving evidence of the last revision, presumably done under his direction (Item 6403). Tyndale continued working to translate portions of the Old Testament from the Hebrew. He ultimately succeeded in finishing the Pentateuch, the book of Jonah (Item 6406), and possibly other historical books of the Old Testament before his execution in 1536. Later editions and revisions (Items 6404, 6405) became an important reference for other English versions of the Bible. These included the Matthew's Bible, the Great Bible, the Coverdale Bible, the Geneva Bible, and the King James Bible.

Case 6400 – Item Diagnostics

6401:	WILLIAM TYNDALE, FRAGMENT OF THE GOSPEL OF ST. MATTHEW, FACSIMILE Ink on paper Cologne, Germany 1525 *On loan from a private collection*	6404:	WILLIAM TYNDALE, NEW TESTAMENT LEAF Ink on paper Antwerp, Belgium 1536 GC.BIB.003837
6402:	WILLIAM TYNDALE, NEW TESTAMENT, FACSIMILE Ink on paper Worms, Germany 1526 GC.BIB.003602	6405:	WILLIAM TYNDALE, *AN EXPOSITION UPON THE V, VI, VII CHAPTERS OF MATTHEW* Ink on paper Antwerp, Belgium 1549 or 1550 GC.PBK.000831
6403:	WILLIAM TYNDALE, NEW TESTAMENT FRAGMENT Ink on paper Antwerp, Belgium 1535 GC.BIB.003598	6406:	WILLIAM TYNDALE, *THE PROPHET JONAS*, FACSIMILE Printed by Merten de Keyser Ink on paper Antwerp, Belgium 1531 GC.BIB.003872

John Knox and Reformation Translations

You have entered John Knox's chapel in Geneva, Switzerland. Listen as this Protestant Reformer and Scottish clergyman presents an overview of some of the earliest translations of the English Bible that followed the printing and translation of William Tyndale's New Testament.

In the sixteenth century, many Protestants were forced to leave their home countries and travel to places where they would be allowed to practice their religious beliefs more freely. Knox served, for a short time, as a minister to a group of exiled English Protestants in Frankfurt, Germany, and later in Geneva, Switzerland.

While living as exiles in Geneva, Knox and his collogues produced their own Bible translation: the Geneva Bible. Their translation was the first complete Bible to be translated into English from the original Hebrew and

Case 6500 – Item Diagnostics

6501:	COVERDALE BIBLE Translated by Myles Coverdale Likely printed by Cervicornus and Soter Ink on paper Probably Cologne, Germany 1535 GC.BIB.003055	6502:	THE NEW TESTAMENT IN LATIN AND ENGLISH, OR COVERDALE'S DIGLOT, FIRST QUARTO EDITION Translated by Myles Coverdale Printed by James Nicolson Ink on paper Southwark, England 1538 GC.BIB.001103

Greek text. The Geneva Bible was also the first English Bible to incorporate versification and to include study notes. It quickly became the preferred translation for English Protestants. Knox is considered the founder of Presbyterianism in Scotland.

Coverdale and the First Printed Bible in English [Case 6500]

While William Tyndale languished in his cell in the Vilvorde Prison, a series of new English Bible translations began to appear. In 1535, Myles Coverdale, an Augustinian friar who was eventually influenced by the works of Martin Luther, translated and produced the first complete English Bible ever printed. Coverdale's Bible (Item 6501), however, was translated from the Latin Vulgate. Since Coverdale was not proficient in Hebrew or Greek, he used Tyndale's New Testament and translations of the Pentateuch and book of Jonah in making his translation. In 1538, Coverdale produced a parallel New Testament (Item 6502) in both English and Latin; the text was printed in two columns on the same page. Coverdale hoped to demonstrate the dependence of his English translation on the Latin. Alongside William Tyndale, Coverdale's footprints can be found in practically every early Protestant English Bible.

During the succession of Queen Mary I, Coverdale was denied the post of Bishop of Exeter due to his involvement in the Reformed cause.

The King's Eyes Are Opened [Case 6600]

In 1537, the first edition of the Bible known as the Matthew's version emerged (Item 6602). "Thomas Matthew" is believed to be a pseudonym for John Rogers, a close and intimate friend of William Tyndale. John Rodgers was the first English Protestant martyred during the reign of Queen Mary I. Like Tyndale, he was burned at the stake. Since Rogers primarily edited what was essentially Tyndale's work in this text, some scholars believe that Thomas Matthew was an alias for Tyndale himself, and that Rogers merely compiled what Tyndale had pre-

Case 6600 – Item Diagnostics

6601:	ALEXANDER JOHNSON, *TYNDALE TRANSLATING THE BIBLE INTO ENGLISH* Oil on canvas England 1854 GC.ART.000362
6602:	THE MATTHEW'S BIBLE Translated by John Rogers Printed by Richard Grafton and Edward Whitchurch Ink on paper Likely Antwerp, Belgium 1537 GC.BIB.003599
6603:	THE GREAT BIBLE Translated by Myles Coverdale Printed by Richard Grafton and Edward Whitchurch Ink on paper London, England 1539 GC.BIB.002904

viously published. The text in the Pentateuch aligns closely to Tyndale's previous work and the New Testament follows with Tyndale's 1535 first edition imprint. Other portions of the Bible (Ezra to the Apocrypha) are clearly reproducing Coverdale's work. Joshua to Chronicles, however, differs so much from Coverdale's translation that these books are thought to be based on manuscript material left behind by William Tyndale. At the request of Thomas Cranmer, Thomas Cromwell issued the King's "most gracious Lycece," making the Matthew's Bible the first English Bible distributed under a Royal License.

Alexander Johnston's depiction of *"Tyndale Translating the Bible into English"* (Item 6601), features John Rogers (standing) and William Tyndale (seated). This work was exhibited at London's Royal Academy in 1854—number 503 in the exhibition.

According to *Foxe's Book of Martyrs*, Tyndale's last words before he was burned at the stake were "Lord, open the king of England's eyes." It would seem Tyndale's prayer was answered posthumously. In 1538, Thomas Cromwell issued an injunction to the clergy by decree of King Henry VIII that "the whole bible of the largest volume to be set up in some convenient place within the said church that you have care of, where as your parishioners may most commodiously resort to the same and read it." In 1539, the first authorized English version, known as the Great Bible (Item 6603), was available to the masses. This text is a revision of the Matthew's Bible. Myles Coverdale, who worked directly under Cromwell's direction, used texts from various Latin translations of the Hebrew, the Vulgate, Erasmus's Latin of the New Testament and the Complutensian Polyglot. The Great Bible is also known as Cromwell's Bible or Cranmer's Bible, since Archbishop Cranmer provided the prologue in the subsequent printings of this Bible.

Case 6700 – Item Diagnostics

6701:	**PARAPHRASE OF ERASMUS ON THE NEW TESTAMENT, VOLUME I**
	Translated by Myles Coverdale, Queen Mary, et al.
	Printed by Edward Whitchurch
	Ink on paper
	London, England
	1548
	GC.BIB.003600.1
6702:	**PARAPHRASE OF ERASMUS ON THE NEW TESTAMENT, VOLUME II**
	Translated by Myles Coverdale, Queen Mary, et al.
	Printed by Edward Whitchurch
	Ink on paper
	London, England
	1548
	GC.BIB.003600.2
6703:	*THE SECOND SERMON OF MASTER HUGH LATIMER, WHICH HE PREACHED BEFORE THE KING'S MAJESTY IN HIS GRACE'S PALACE...*
	Printed by John Day
	Ink on paper
	Westminster, London
	1549
	GC.PBK.000303

The Oxford Martyrs [Case 6700]

During the reign of Queen Mary Tudor, known to Protestants as "Bloody Mary," hundreds of people were sentenced to death, due to their opposing religious convictions. Mary was determined to reinstate Roman Catholicism as the state's official religion after her father, King Henry VIII, broke from Rome and declared himself to be the head of the Church of England, despite having once been declared "Fidei Defensor" (Defender of the Faith) by the pope. King Edward VI, Mary's half-brother and successor to Henry VIII, was raised under the tutelage and sermons of Hugh Latimer (Item 6703) and the influences of the Archbishop of Canterbury, Thomas Cranmer, both Protestants. Consequently, an advancement of the English Reformation pushed forward with official religious practices looking more Protestant and less Catholic during King Edward VI's six year reign. At the age of 15, "the boy king" contracted a terminal disease. In an effort to thwart future attempts to reinstate Catholic doctrine to a now Protestant English church, before Edward's death the "Devise for Succession Act" was drawn by Edward and his council naming Edward's cousin Lady Jane Grey as heir to the throne, thus preventing his half-sisters Mary and Elizabeth from inheriting the crown.

Following the death of King Edward, Mary deposed the nine-day queen Lady Jane Grey and had her beheaded for treason. Then the Marian persecutions began. Mary's reign instilled fear throughout the Protestant lands of England. Many Protestants fled to Geneva, Switzerland, which had a more religiously tolerant environment. Some Protestants converted to Catholicism only to denounce that faith following Queen Mary's death. Three former Protestant Bishops, Hugh Latimer, Nicholas Ridley, and the Archbishop of Canterbury, Thomas Cranmer, were tried under Mary's reign in 1555. Latimer and Ridley were burned together, where it is reported that Latimer said to Ridley, "Play the man, Master Ridley; we shall this day light such a candle, by God's grace, in England, as I trust shall never be put out." Queen Mary attempted to extinguish any flame the Protestant Reformation may have sparked, including her own translation of the Gospel of St. John published in the English Translation of Erasmus' New Testament Paraphrase (Items 6701, 6702). In 1556, the Archbishop of Canterbury, Thomas Cranmer, was burned at the stake. Cranmer was forcibly persuaded to recant his Protestant views. Though he signed a recantation, Cranmer refused to affirm these views publicly as he stood before his former congregation at University Church, Oxford, and was sentenced to death. Cranmer did promise publicly that "forasmuch as my hand hath offended, writing contrary to my heart, therefore my hand shall first be punished; for when I come to the fire, it shall first be burned." During his execution, Cranmer leaned forward and placed his offending hand into the fire first.

Case 6800 – Item Diagnostics

6801:	**GENEVA BIBLE** Translated by William Whittingham, Anthony Gilby, et al. Printed by Rouland Hall Ink on paper Geneva, Switzerland 1560 GC.BIB.003034
6802:	**WILLIAM FULKE, *A DEFENSE OF THE SINCERE AND TRUE TRANSLATIONS OF THE HOLY SCRIPTURES INTO THE ENGLISH TONGUE*** Printed by Henrie Bynneman Ink on paper London, England 1583 GC.PBK.000315
6803:	**HUGH BROUGHTON, *DANIEL, HIS CHALDIE VISIONS...*** Printed by Richard Field and Gabriel Simson Ink on paper London, England 1596 GC.PBK.000830
6804:	**THE BISHOPS' BIBLE** Translated by Matthew Parker Printed by Richard Jugge Ink on paper London, England 1569 GC.BIB.001158
6805:	**THE RHEIMS NEW TESTAMENT** Translated by Gregory Martin Printed by John Fogny Ink on paper Rheims, France 1582 GC.BIB.003035

Protestants, Catholics, and English Bibles   [Case 6800]

The Geneva Bible (Item 6801) is the first complete Bible to be translated into English from the original Hebrew and Greek text. First published in 1560, this edition is the result of English Puritans and French Protestant dissidents who fled their homeland seeking refuge from religious persecution. William Whittingham, Myles Coverdale, John Calvin, Theodore Beza, and John Knox are a few of the theologians and scholars responsible for this translation. Considered the Bible of the Protestant Reformation, this translation was the first English Bible to contain numbered chapters and verses, printed with Roman type set, and extensive theological study notes. The study notes were perhaps the most controversial section for the crown and the officials in the Church of England, as it called into question the absolute power of the monarchy and the church establishment. For example, one note on the Book of Daniel says, Daniel "disobeyed the king's wicked commandment in order to obey God, and so he did no injury to the king, who ought to command nothing by which God, would be dishonored." This controversy spurred additional commentaries and independent translations of the books of the Bible into English, such as Hugh Broughton's *Daniel, His Chaldie Visions* (Item 6803). Broughton was a Puritan scholar, who was excluded from the translation committee of the King James Bible, which he would later vehemently oppose. The Geneva Bible was an extremely influential translation. William Shakespeare quoted from the Geneva Bible over 2,000 times. John Bunyan read this edition while imprisoned in the Bedford County Gaol (jail). And it is the Bible that was brought to the "New World" by the Pilgrims and Puritans.

Contention grew over the Calvinistic overtones of the Geneva Bible's study notes. In 1568, the Church of England authorized a new translation: The Bishops' Bible (Item 6804), so-named as it was produced under the direction of Matthew Parker, Archbishop of Canterbury. The Bishops' Bible was printed with a more ecclesiastical language but contained no study notes, and it was used as the basis for the King James translation.

In 1582, the first Catholic New Testament printed in English was produced in Rheims, France (Item 6805). Noted scholar Father Gregory Martin translated this text entirely from the Latin Vulgate with comparisons to the Greek. Puritan attempts to vilify the translation, such as William Fulke's *A Defense of the English Translation* (Item 6802), backfired instead making it more popular amongst Catholics. In 1609–1610, the Catholic English translation of the Old Testament was printed in Douai, France. The complete work is known as the Douay-Rheims version. The translators of the 1611 King James Bible used the Rheims New Testament. They adopted many of Father Martin's phrases, vocabulary, and characteristics of expressions.

The King James Bible: A Translation to Unite the English

In 1604, King James I called a conference to Hampton Court to try to address various concerns of the Puritans and the state-supported Church of England. The king and his bishops were unhappy with the Geneva Bible and its annotations, though it was very popular among the Puritans. Their alternative, the Great Bible, was large, unwieldy, and expensive. On the second day of the conference, the king embraced the idea of producing a new translation to satisfy both parties' concerns. This new translation was a group effort, involving several committees and roughly 47 scholars. (The actual number is uncertain.) The scholars were instructed to find the best translations, using the 1602 edition of the Bishops' Bible as their base text, and to compare them with the most reliable texts of the Bible in the original languages. The entire process took seven years.

The New Testament committee met to discuss their final draft in the Jerusalem Chamber at Westminster Abbey. The gallery you are standing in is a scaled replica of that room. Decorative tapestries flank a large fireplace on one wall, while a portrait of King James I hangs on the opposite wall. In the center of the room, a large table is strewn with sources likely used by the committee members.

If you listen closely, you can hear the translators debating the pros and cons of various translations. Their conversation illustrates how closely tied the process of translation is to commentary, interpretation, and theological perspective. Despite the difficulties of their work, the translators of the King James Bible succeeded in producing the most printed, most quoted, and most influential English translation of the Bible to date.

Scholarship, Texts, and Translation: Sources Used by the King James Translators [Case 6900]

These texts illustrate some of the academic sources that were beginning to become available at the time of the translation of the King James Bible. Many of these are polyglots, or books which contain the text of the Bible in multiple languages running alongside one another (Items 6901, 6902, 6903, 6904, 6905). By comparing different translations of the same passage, Bible translators are able to get a better sense of the meaning of the biblical text. For example, in this case you see New Testament text with commentary by Theodore Beza, John Calvin's successor (Item 6905). In these marginal notes, Beza discusses the textual validity of 1 John 5:7 at great length. Based on the lack of evidence in the earliest Greek manuscripts, other ancient versions of the book, and the quotation of this verse by Church Fathers, he concludes that the verse was not original to the ancient biblical text. He still includes it, however, underscoring once again the struggle that scholars and translators face—whether Jewish, Protestant, Catholic, or Orthodox—as they deal with theological traditions that do not correspond to the textual evidence.

It is likely that the committee of scholars who translated the King James Bible consulted many of these texts during their translation process, the main source being the Bishops' Bible (Item 6907). Forty unbound copies of the 1602 Bishops' Bible were issued to the members of the king's translation committee, and several still survive with the translators' notes. Another main source was the sixteenth-century Greek New Testament edition by

Case 6900 – Item Diagnostics

6901:	**STEPHANUS, NEW TESTAMENT, VOLUME I** Containing the Latin Vulgate, Original Greek, and Erasmus's Latin Edition, respectively Printed by Robert Estienne Ink on paper Geneva, Switzerland 1551 GC.BIB.003725.1	6905:	**THEODORE BEZA, NEW TESTAMENT, FOURTH EDITION** Printed by Henri Estienne Ink on paper Geneva, Switzerland 1598 GC.BIB.000888
6902:	**OLD TESTAMENT IN HEBREW AND LATIN, ILLUSTRATIONS BY TREMELLIUS AND JUNIUS** Printed by George Bishop Ink on paper London, England 1579/1580 GC.BIB.000974	6906:	**GREEK NEW TESTAMENT** Printed by Bonaventure and Abraham Elzevir Ink on paper Leiden, Holland 1633 GC.BIB.001186
6903:	**THE PLANTIN POLYGLOT** Printed by Christopher Plantin Ink on paper Antwerp, Belgium 1584 GC.BIB.001115	6907:	**THE BISHOPS' BIBLE** Printed by Robert Barker Ink on paper London, England 1602 GC.BIB.001056
6904:	**NEW TESTAMENT POLYGLOT, IN GREEK AND LATIN** Ink on paper Paris, France 1584 GC.BIB.001044		

Case 7000 – Item Diagnostics

7001:	**KING JAMES NEW TESTAMENT WITH THE BOOK OF COMMON PRAYER, FIRST EDITION** Printed by Robert Barker Ink on paper London, England 1611 GC.BIB.002908
7002:	**THE PSALMS OF KING DAVID, TRANSLATED BY KING JAMES** Printed by William Turner Ink on paper Oxford, England 1631 GC.BIB.002899
7003:	**GREAT "HE" KING JAMES BIBLE, FIRST EDITION** Printed by Robert Barker Ink on paper London, England 1611 GC.BIB.001442
7004:	**MATTHEW SUTCLIFFE, *THE SUPPLICATION OF CERTAIN MASS-PRIESTS FALSELY CALLED CATHOLICS*** Printed by George Eld and Valentine Simmes Ink on paper London, England 1604 GC.BIB.002833
7005:	**GREAT "SHE" BIBLE** Printed by Robert Barker Ink on paper London, England 1613/1611 GC.BIB.000271

Erasmus, which was later given the name *"textus receptus,"* or "the received text," by Daniel Heinsius (d. 1655) in the preface to Bonaventure and Abraham Elzevier's Greek New Testament edition of 1633 (Item 6906).

King James and His Bible   [Case 7000]

King James I was incredibly interested in biblical studies. He wrote on theological matters and translated portions of the text before becoming king of England (Item 7004). Some of these writings, like his translation of the Psalms, did not see publication until after his death, but enjoyed great popularity, serving as a propagandistic merging of the inspired reign of David with James and the Stuart Dynasty (Item 7002).

Of all these endeavors, none have remained as popular as the King James Version of the Bible. After years of labor overseeing the translation committee, James commissioned Robert Barker of London to see to the widespread printing and dispersion of the new "authorized" version of the Bible in 1611. This version was to replace all former liturgical texts and supplant all other English versions that were currently being used. In the first year, the Bible was produced in one and two volume editions. The two volume editions contained the Old and the New Testaments, respectively (Item 7001). These editions were affordable and portable, resulting in much wear and tear. Very few remain today. The one volume folio editions have survived in greater numbers.

After the initial printing of the first folio edition, the committee made a translation revision to Ruth 3:15. In this verse, the subject of the sentence is somewhat ambiguous, so in the first edition printing the phrase was rendered, "*he* went into the citie." Afterwards, they decided that the subject is meant to be Ruth, changing it to "*she* went into the citie." Therefore, the first edition is known as the "He" Bible, and the second edition the "She" Bible (Items 7003, 7005).

Pulpit Bibles: Great Folio Editions of the King James Bible   [Case 7100]

The Bibles in this case are third and fourth edition, large format folios, intended primarily for pulpit use (Items 7101, 7102). These editions from 1617 and 1634 are based on the original translation, but all translations inevitably require revision, and the King James Version was no exception. In 1638, a "Standard" edition was created, which would remain unchanged for the next 100 years. The majority of modern KJV editions follow the Oxford edition of 1769.

Case 7100 – Item Diagnostics

7101:	**KING JAMES BIBLE, THIRD FOLIO EDITION** Printed by Robert Barker Ink on paper London, England 1617 GC.BIB.000205	**7102:**	**KING JAMES BIBLE, FOURTH FOLIO EDITION** Printed by Robert Barker Ink on paper London, England 1634 GC.BIB.002882

Smaller Editions and Private Use   [Case 7200]

While the large folio editions were for church use, the smaller versions were intended for private use. High demand for these portable, affordable versions expanded the printing base from one shop to many. Robert Barker remained the chief printer for years, but eventually Cambridge and others began printing their own editions. This case contains examples of smaller editions from these presses.

Case 7200 – Item Diagnostics

7201:	**THE KING JAMES BIBLE, FIRST SMALL FOLIO** Printed by Robert Barker Ink on paper London, England 1616 GC.BIB.000874	**7205:**	**THE KING JAMES BIBLE** Printed by John Bill and Christopher Barker Ink on paper London, England 1676 GC.BIB.002434
7202:	**BOOK OF COMMON PRAYER AND BIBLE, WITH ILLUSTRATIONS** Printed by Thomas Guy Ink on paper London, England 1682 GC.BIB.000889	**7206-7:**	**THE KING JAMES BIBLE, 2 VOLUMES** Ink on paper England 1695 GC.BIB.000829.1-.2
7203:	**THE KING JAMES BIBLE** Printed by Thomas Buck and Roger Daniel Ink on paper Cambridge, England 1637 GC.BIB.001004	**7206-7:**	**THE KING JAMES BIBLE, 2 VOLUMES** Ink on paper England 1695 GC.BIB.000829.1-.2
7204:	**THE NEW TESTAMENT** Printed by Robert Barker Ink on paper London, England 1637 GC.BIB.001722	**7208:**	**THE KING JAMES BIBLE** Printed by Robert Barker Ink on paper London, England 1613 GC.BIB.000221

Bible Translation in the Modern Era

The history of Bible translation for the last four hundred years is closely connected to the modern Christian missionary movement, which emphasizes translation as a primary method of spreading Christianity. When English clergyman John Eliot translated the Bible into the native dialect of the Algonquin tribe of Massachusetts in the 1650s, he did so for missionary purposes, saying, "Until we have Bibles, we are not furnished to carry the Gospel unto them for we have no means to carry religion thither, saving the Scriptures."

The British and Foreign Bible Society was formed in 1804 to encourage "wider circulation and use" of the Bible. Shortly thereafter, similar organizations were formed in countries around the world, including Switzerland (1804), Finland (1812), Russia (1813), Hungary (1812), the Netherlands (1814), Sweden (1815), and the United States (1816). These organizations funded Bible translation and production on a much wider scale than had ever been done before. The primary way they accomplished this was to send missionaries to communities were the Bible was not available in the local language. These missionaries then spent years living with the locals, learning their language, and eventually producing translations of portions of the Bible for their use.

This process continues today, as Christian missionary organizations work to make the Bible available in every known language. Of the 7,000 languages known to be actively spoken in the world today, more than 500 have complete Bible translations. Another 2,300 languages have active translation projects currently underway.

Case 7300 – Item Diagnostics

7301:	**THE GOSPEL OF MATTHEW, MOHAWK LANGUAGE TRANSLATION** Translated by H.A. Hill and revised by John A. Wilkes Young Men's Bible Society of New York Ink on paper New York, New York 1836 GC.BIB.002816
7302:	**THE GOSPEL OF LUKE, SENECA LANGUAGE TRANSLATION** Translated by T.S. Harris American Bible Society Ink on paper New York, New York 1829 GC.BIB.003594
7303:	**THE NEW TESTAMENT, DAKOTA LANGUAGE TRANSLATION** Translated by S.R. Riggs American Bible Society Ink on paper New York, New York 1886 GC.BIB.002811

Native American Bible Translations   [Case 7300]

When European settlers first landed in America, they encountered a number of different Native American tribes, each of which had distinct cultures, languages, and religions. The first translation of the Bible into the language of Native Americans was also the first complete Bible printed in America: the Eliot Indian Bible. English Clergyman John Eliot translated the Bible into the Natick dialect of the region's Algonquin tribes so that he could use the book as an evangelistic tool in preaching to the local Native American population. Samuel Green and his assistant Marmaduke Johnson in Cambridge, Massachusetts, printed the first edition between 1660 and 1663. Most copies of this Bible were never used for evangelistic purposes, however, but ended up in the collections of Europeans who were attracted to the novelty of the language.

The nineteenth century saw a huge influx of Bible translations among the native people groups of the Americas. Bibles were translated into the languages of the many different Indian nations of North America, such as the Mohawks (Item 7301) and the Seneca (Item 7302) of the Northeast, and the Dakota of the northern Midwest (Item 7303). In many instances, missionaries attempting to translate the Bible were not only mastering new languages, but also giving them a written form for the first time.

Modern Translations in Africa [Case 7400]

The African continent is home to some 3,000 native languages, split between half a dozen language families. African missionaries, like the missionaries to the Native Americans, often had to create written languages for their translations. This was the case with David Jones's translation of the New Testament into Malagasy, the language of Madagascar (Item 7402). Jones, a Welsh missionary with the London Missionary Society, worked with King Radama I of Madagascar to develop the orthography, or writing system, for the language.

Case 7400 – Item Diagnostics

7401:	THE NEW TESTAMENT, TSHILUBA LANGUAGE TRANSLATION
	Bible Society of Congo
	Ink on paper
	Leopoldville, Democratic Republic of Congo
	1962
	GC.BIB.001234
7402:	THE NEW TESTAMENT, MALAGASY LANGUAGE TRANSLATION
	Translated by David Jones and David Griffiths
	Signed by printer, Edward Baker
	London Missionary Society
	Ink on paper
	Antananarivo, Madagascar
	1830
	GC.BIB.002868

Translating the Bible for India [Case 7500]

This case features Bibles translated into different languages spoken on the Indian subcontinent. One of the most important figures in the nineteenth-century missionary efforts on the Indian subcontinent was William Carey, an English minister who helped found the Baptist Missionary Society. After serving as minister at a number of churches in England, Carey moved to India in 1793. He originally settled in Calcutta, but moved north to Serampore after a few years due to problems with the East India Company. In Serampore, Carey established a

Case 7500 – Item Diagnostics

7501:	SELECTIONS FROM THE BIBLE IN THE MARATHI LANGUAGE	7503:	THE BIBLE, BENGALI LANGUAGE TRANSLATION
	Translated by Vaidyanath Sarma and William Carey		Translated by J. Wenger and W. Yates
	American Missionary Press		Printed for the Bible Translation Society, at the Baptist Mission Press
	Ink on paper		Ink on paper
	Bombay, India		Calcutta, India
	1817–1820		1853
	GC.BIB.000694		GC.BIB.000997
7502:	THE BOOK OF GENESIS AND PART OF EXODUS, SANSKRIT LANGUAGE TRANSLATION	7504:	THE NEW TESTAMENT, HINDUWEE, OR HIGH HINDI, LANGUAGE TRANSLATION
	Translated by Calcutta Baptist Missionaries		British and Foreign Bible Society
	Printed for the Bible Translation Society at the Baptist Mission Press		Ink on paper
	Ink on paper		London, England
	Calcutta, India		1860
	1843		GC.BIB.001599
	GC.BIB.001603		

school and a print shop where he produced a number of the first translations of the Bible in various Indian dialects, including Marathi (Item 7501), Sanskrit (Item 7502), and Bengali (Item 7503).

The Bible in East Asia   [Case 7600]

This case features Bibles translated into different languages spoken in the Asian countries of China (Items 7601, 7603, 7604) and Japan (Item 7602). There has been a modern missionary presence in the Far East since the sixteenth century. Initially many were Catholic missionaries, but they were soon joined by Christians from the Orthodox and Protestant denominations. As part of their evangelistic efforts, missionaries began working on translations of the Bible in the local languages. The writing systems of most Asian languages, however, were so complex that the first translations of the Bible in these languages were produced using woodblocks (Items 7601, 7602).

Case 7600 – Item Diagnostics

7601:	THE NEW TESTAMENT, IN ENGLISH AND MANDARIN	7603:	THE NEW TESTAMENT, CHIN KAMHAU DIALECT TRANSLATION
	Presbyterian Mission Press		Translated by J.H. Cope
	American Bible Society		British and Foreign Bible Society
	Ink on paper		Ink on paper
	Shanghai, China		Rangoon, Burma
	1885		1945
	GC.BIB.001421		GC.BIB.000994
7602:	THE NEW TESTAMENT, IN JAPANESE	7604:	THE NEW TESTAMENT, KUOYU LANGUAGE TRANSLATION
	Bible Societies' Commission for Japan		American Bible Society
	Ink on paper		Ink on paper
	Japan		United States
	1896		1944
	GC.BIB.001930		GC.BIB.002958

Thousands of Islands, Thousands of Languages   [Case 7700]

The Pacific Ocean contains between 20,000 and 30,000 islands, most of which are located below the Tropic of Cancer in the South Pacific. This case features Bibles translated into the local languages of Tahiti (Item 7701), Hawaii (Item 7702), New Zealand (Item 7703), and British New Guinea (Item 7704). The native societies in this region are thousands of years old, but the first European contact with these islands did not take place until the eighteenth-century explorations of James Cook. In the following century, the London Missionary Society sent numerous missionaries to live and work on these islands, with Bibles being one obvious product of their time.

Case 7700 – Item Diagnostics

7701:	**THE BIBLE, EARLY TAHITIAN LANGUAGE TRANSLATION** Translated by Henry Noot, Revised by William Howe and Thomas Joseph British and Foreign Bible Society London, England 1847 GC.BIB.001250	7703:	**THE NEW TESTAMENT, MAORI LANGUAGE TRANSLATION** Translated and Revised by W. Williams, first Bishop of Waiapu, New Zealand British and Foreign Bible Society London, England 1852 GC.PBK.000453
7702:	**THE BIBLE, HAWAIIAN LANGUAGE TRANSLATION** American Bible Society Hawaii 1884 GC.BIB.000332	7704:	**THE FOUR GOSPELS, KIWAI LANGUAGE TRANSLATION OF BRITISH NEW GUINEA** British and Foreign Bible Society Ink on paper Commonwealth of Australia 1947 GC.BIB.001590

Movement 4—Impact

Throughout history, no one book has had a more significant impact on the world than the Bible. Its influence has touched every sphere—from art and music to philosophy and science to cultural and religious practices.

Biblical themes have provided inspiration for some of the greatest artistic masterpieces of all time, including Leonardo Da Vinci's *The Last Supper*, Handel's *Messiah*, and John Milton's *Paradise Lost*. The Bible is also the central text for two major world religions, greatly influencing their rituals and liturgical practices. In America, the Bible has had an incredible impact on the country's history and popular culture. Its words can be found inscribed on the walls of the Library of Congress and immortalized in the lyrics of "The Battle Hymn of the Republic."

This section presents just a few of the many reasons why the Bible is widely considered the most influential book ever written.

The Bible and Jewish Liturgy

Liturgy involves the words, rituals, customs, and processes for how public religious worship is conducted. Liturgical practices reflect the beliefs of those who enact them, often drawing on the sacred texts of their religion for instruction and inspiration.

In the Jewish tradition, liturgical practice draws heavily from the Tanakh, particularly the rules for worshiping in the Temple detailed in the Torah. Demonstrations of faith, such as acts of worship, often incorporate the use of material objects. The vessels, implements, and clothing used in Jewish worship and ceremony to express the rich, meaningful symbols, and ritual actions of their beliefs are called Judaica. Such implements serve as a material record of specific rites and rituals. The displays in this gallery reflect these liturgical customs of feasting, dress, prayer, and reverence for the sacred text.

It is important to note that Christian traditions overlap, in many ways, with Jewish liturgical practices. This relationship found its most literal expression in the formation and architecture of the early Church during the Byzantine Period, when Christian sacred spaces were superimposed on top of earlier sites of Jewish worship. Some even mimic the architectural footprint of the earlier structures. When you are finished here, step through to the next gallery to learn more about Christian liturgical practice, including the ways in which it draws from its Jewish origins.

The Jewish Calendar and Feast Holidays   [Case 7800]

In many cultures, feasting and dining may be associated with a specific season or holiday. The communal meal can also be a form of fellowship. In Judaism, there are numerous *haggim*, or holidays, which bring both family and community together for a variety of reasons. The most frequent occasion for such gatherings is the Sabbath. It is also regarded as one of the most important, being the sole occasion for weekly ritual observance commanded by God.

> *Remember the Sabbath day by keeping it holy. Six days you shall labor and do all your work, but the seventh day is a Sabbath to the Lord your God. On it you shall not do any work, neither you, nor your son or daughter, nor your male or female servant, nor your animals, nor any foreigner residing in your towns. For in six days the Lord made the heavens and the earth, the sea, and all that is in them, but he rested on the seventh day. Therefore the Lord blessed the Sabbath day and made it holy.* (Exodus 20:8-11, NIV).

Erev Shabbat is the evening prior to the Sabbath, when the appearance of the first star marks the commencement of the Sabbath. Observant Jews gather at this time, typically following a prayer service. Various implements are set on the table, such as the *kiddush* cup (Item 7801) shown here. This vessel is used while reciting the *kiddush*, a prayer of blessing and thanks followed by the communal drinking of wine (though sometimes substituted for grape juice). *Pesach* (Passover, or Feast of Unleavened Bread), *Rosh Hashanah* (Jewish New Year, or Feast of Trumpets), and *Sukkot* (Feast of Tabernacles) are some of the holidays in the Jewish calendar which incorporate different types of food for ritualistic observance. All of these are marked by the use of utensils or decorative wares that serve to illustrate the purpose of the feast and its meaning for the participants.

Case 7800 – Item Diagnostics

7801:	KIDDUSH CUP	7804:	PLATTER FOR SEDER
	Silver		Painted ceramic
	Italy		Italy
	19th century		1880
	GC.JUD.000857.1-.2		GC.CER.000204
7802:	PASSOVER *AFIKOMEN* (MATZAH) BAG	7805:	*BESOMIM* (SPICE CONTAINER)
	Embroidered cloth		Silver
	Israel		Augsburg, Germany
	Circa 1920		18th century
	GC.TXT.000195		GC.JUD.000850.1-.2
7803:	PASSOVER *AFIKOMEN* (MATZAH) COVER	7806:	*BESOMIM* (SPICE CONTAINER)
	Embroidered cloth		Silver
	Hungary		Galicia, Ukraine
	1900		18th century
	GC.TXT.000169		GC.JUD.000874

Devotion through Dress [Case 7900]

Within many faith groups and denominations, there are uniquely crafted vestments that distinguish laity from religious leaders and authorities. It is believed that the temple priests from antiquity would have worn specific robes. Since the destruction of the Temple in AD 70, however, the Jewish community has shifted away from a centralized religious authority. Modern Judaism makes no such distinctions. There are no priests—only rabbis, who serve as teachers. These figures do not possess any executive authority as religious leaders, though they may rise to positions of political influence within their community, such as a chief rabbi. Even then, their dress may not reflect an elevated status.

Case 7900 – Item Diagnostics

7901:	*TALLIT KATAN* (MAN'S UNDERGARMENT)	7903:	*TEFILLIN* (PHYLACTERIES)
	Cotton		Leather
	Czech Republic		Probably Israel
	19th century		20th century
	GC.TXT.000205		GC.JUD.000590.1-.2
7902:	HEAD COVERING	7904:	*CHALITZAH* (DIVORCE) SHOE
	Silk		Leather
	Hungary		Germany
	Circa 1900		19th century
	GC.TXT.000152		GC.OBJ.000326

Generally, any variance in the aesthetics of a Jewish man's or woman's garb is influenced by their gender and culture. There are costumes and textiles specific to different regions of the world that have permeated the culture of dress within local Jewish communities. Thus, a Jewish bride in Yemen may look very different from one in Poland. The aesthetics of a garment may also be influenced by the function of the piece. Note the long tassels on

Item 7901. These are called *tzitzit* and are attached to a man's undergarment. These are designed to graze the body when in motion. Their continual contact is intended to bring awareness and focus to the knots on each. Not only does the Torah command that these be worn, it also instructs that through their use, one will be reminded of and present in their *mitzvot*, or commandments from God.

Exegesis   [Case 8000]

Faith, ritual, and worship are all informed by interpretation of scripture. Such examination and critique is known as exegesis. Since antiquity, this practice has influenced the way the Jewish people relate to their doctrine. *Peshers*, or commentaries on biblical writings, have existed at least since the time of the Second Temple, if not prior—as exhibited by the numerous *pesherim* discovered at Qumran. Such interpretive writings continue into the modern era, demonstrating varied perspectives from all communities. For example, the tenth-century Jewish philosopher Saadia Gaon was famous for having introduced an Arabized interpretation of scripture, relying heavily on logic and philosophy, which is still apparent in biblical hermeneutics today.

Case 8000 – Item Diagnostics

8001:	COMMENTARY ON THE BOOK OF ESTHER, IN HEBREW
	Ink on paper
	Iraq
	11th century
	GC.MS.000765
8002:	KARAITE PRAYER BOOK
	Ink on paper
	Egypt
	13th–15th century
	GC.PPR.010107.1-.4
8003:	TAJ TORAH, IN HEBREW AND ARABIC
	Ink on paper
	Yemen
	16th century
	GC.MS.000472

By contrast, a contemporary Jewish sect known as the Karaites rejected any philosophical interpretations that detracted from the strictly literal interpretation of the biblical text. Item 8002 is a prayer book that would have been used by a Karaite Jew. The greatest schism remaining between rabbinical Jews and the much smaller minority of Karaites centers on the belief regarding the tradition of an oral law that passes down from the patriarchs generation by generation. Karaites maintain that any extra-biblical law not recorded in the five books of Moses is a product of men and is thus imperfect. For Rabbinical Jews, this is a challenge to their practice of exegesis and interpretive thinking that produced such written works as the *Mishnah* and *Gemara*, the codification of all laws and regulations that define rabbinical Jewish life. Naturally, these two branches of Judaism look very different in practice.

Apotropaic Practices   [Case 8100]

Amulets are objects that are either worn by or placed nearby one seeking protection, like a talisman. These protective objects are believed to shield the bearer of such objects from evil spirits and misfortune. The "evil eye," seen most notably throughout Anatolia (modern Turkey), is a product of this philosophy. In the Jewish world, the *hamsa* is the most prevalent apotropaic (warding magic) symbol, such as the two shown here (Items 8106, 8107).

Earlier amulets would have been made much like the more modern necklaces found in Middle Eastern bazaars and curio shops, with rolled scrolls encased inside tubular pendants. Sometimes these scrolls contained biblical excerpts. Note Item 8101, shown here. The inscription includes a quotation from Deuteronomy 6:4-7.

Line 1: Spell for the existence of the son of Theodorah. Tell [them to them.?>>] I adjure[-]
Line 2: And the demons who are afflicting the existence of the son of Theodorah. [-]
Line 3: That you are dead, the words and all that the Heavens have told to the man [-]
Line 4: << Listen, Israel, YYYY our God is one Lord. Va[cat]
Line 5: You must love the Lord your God with all your heart and with all [your soul and with all]
Line 6: Your strength. May these words that I [enjoin on you] today, stay
Line 7: In your heart. And you shall teach them to your children and you shall [. . .]

In late antiquity, there was a widespread practice of divination, whereby incantations would be coupled with prayers. Such appeals would be made to specific angels for blessings, good fortunes, wellness, and healing. These incantations were often inscribed on items like this silver amulet or, as we find in Mesopotamia, on ceramics (Items 8104, 8105).

Case 8100 – Item Diagnostics

8101:	**LAMELLA**	8105:	**INCANTATION JUG**
	Silver		Ink on ceramic base
	Israel		Sassanian Asoristan
	4th–7th century		5th–8th century
	GC.AMU.000134		gc.fic.000003
8102:	**STYLUS**	8106:	**HAMSA**
	Silver		Silver
	Roman Palestine		Tunisia
	1st–3rd century		20th century
	GC.OBJ.000145		GC.AMU.000231
8103:	**LAMELLA**	8107:	**HAMSA**
	Gold		Silver
	Levant		Morocco
	Date Unknown		20th century
	This item is currently under research with the Green Scholars Initiative		GC.AMU.000226
	GC.AMU.000135.1-.2		
8104:	**INCANTATION BOWL**		
	Ink on ceramic base		
	Sassanian Asoristan		
	5th–8th century		
	GC.CER.000518		

The Sefer Torah   [Case 8200]

The Torah is central to the Jewish world, shaping the way in which the religiously observant engage with text. Much like the Christian world, the cultures of faith within Judaism are many and vary from one tradition to another. This variance of culture comes from the regional norms of each diaspora community. The three major communities are *Ashkenazi* (European), *Sepharadi* (Spanish and North African), and *Mizrahi* (Middle Eastern). Each produce scrolls with a slightly different technique and style of writing.

Ashkenazim is the term traditionally used to identify those communities of Ashkenaz, or Rhineland in Germany. Saadia Gaon, a prominent Jewish sage of the tenth century, identified Ashkenaz as a region falling within the Slavic territories of Eastern and Western Europe. Item 8201 has been identified as *Ashkenazi* based on its parchment material as well as the style of the Hebrew characters.

Sephardim is the term traditionally used to identify those communities of Sfarád, or Spain. Because of Spain's continuous cultural engagement with northern Africa throughout time, this term has come to encompass the historic Jewish communities of the Maghreb, including Morocco, Algeria, and Tunisia in particular. Thus, their culture is heavily influenced by the local tastes and aesthetics of the region. Their scrolls are frequently created with a *gvil*, or suede like leather (Item 8202), versus the crisper parchment of the Ashkenazi style.

Case 8200 – Item Diagnostics

8201:	TORAH SCROLL
	Ink on parchment
	Northern Italy or Germany
	Mid-14th century
	GC.SCR.001181
8202:	TORAH SCROLL
	Ink on gvil
	North Africa
	17th century
	GC.SCR.001681
8203:	TORAH SCROLL
	Ink on gvil
	Yemen
	15th–16th century
	GC.SCR.003691

Mirzahim, meaning "of the east," is the term traditionally used to identify those Jewish communities living within Arabized western Asia, as well as the non-Arab Islamic regions of central Asia. The most commonly recognized group to whom this term is attributed is the Babylonian community of Iraq. Since ancient Israel's exile from Judah, as recounted in both biblical narratives and Babylonian texts alike, there has been a Jewish presence in Iraq. This community thrived in late antiquity and even through the Islamic age, with the founding of two prominent Talmudic academies in Pumbedita (near modern Fallujah) and Sura (located further south on the Euphrates River). Another population sometimes associated with these communities of the old world is the Jewish community in Yemen. Centuries ago, many Jews populated the Arabian Peninsula and formed a strong trade in jewels from the port cities lining the Red Sea. Yemenite scrolls are also produced with the gvil of North African Jews, but their writing style is distinct. Note the small spirals incorporated into the text of Item 8203. These are an archaic version of the Hebrew letter *"peh"* which continued into modern times.

Adornment [Case 8300]

Judaica consists of literature, objects, artistic, and ritualistic items pertaining to Jewish life, particularly historical items. Within this broad base of material culture, there are varieties of accessories and implements used specifically for shrouding, adorning, and reading from the *Torah*. As with the *Seferot Torah* in this gallery, regional varieties may be distinguished by their use of material and aesthetic.

Most *Torah* scrolls, irrespective of community, have some kind of barrier for protection as a base upon which additional decoration may be added, such as embroidery, precious metals, and sometimes jewels. These protective apparatuses can be purely functional, like a simple wimple, or they can be highly decorative. The Torah ark in this case (Item 8301) serves for both protecting and adorning. On top of these arks one often finds finials with decorative motifs and bells (Item 8303), possibly intended to recreate the sound of the bells from the Temple priests' robes. Exodus 28:31-35 mentions these in great description:

Make the robe of the ephod entirely of blue cloth, with an opening for the head in its center. There shall be a woven edge like a collar around this opening, so that it will not tear. Make pomegranates of blue, purple and scarlet yarn around the hem of the robe, with gold bells between them. The gold bells and the pomegranates are to alternate around the hem of the robe. Aaron must wear it when he ministers. The sound of the bells will be heard when he enters the Holy Place before the Lord and when he comes out, so that he will not die. (NIV)

Case 8300 – Item Diagnostics

8301:	*TIK* (ARK) WITH *RIMMONIM* (FINIALS) Velvet and metal; silver Egypt 20th century GC.ARK.000847, GC.ARK.000854.1-.2	8305:	*TAS* (SHIELD) Silver Slovakia Early 20th century GC.JUD.000877.1-.2
8302:	TORAH MANTLE Silk and cotton European 19th century GC.FIC.000014	8306:	*YAD* (POINTER) Silver Austria 19th century GC.JUD.000863
8303:	*RIMMONIM* (FINIALS) Silver Morocco Probably 20th century GC.ARK.000857.1-.2	8307:	*YAD* (POINTER) Silver France 19th century GC.JUD.000865
8304:	BOOK COVER Silver Austria 19th century GC.JUD.000717	8308:	*YAD* (POINTER) Silver Netherlands 19th century GC.ARK.000799

A *yad*, or Torah pointer, is another form of adornment, rooted in necessity (Items 8306, 8307, 8308). In Judaism, it is believed that God communicates through the written word. Thus, interaction with and handling of Torah scrolls is an act piety and devotion. As such, great care is taken not to defile the written word of God through human touch, rendering that which is holy impure. A *yad* is used to point at the scroll, so its reader can easily follow the text while reading it without touching the scroll itself. In recent times, printed Hebrew Bibles have begun replacing some use of hand written scrolls for personal ease of use and portability. These too can often come with some form of decorative encasement (Item 8304).

The Bible and Christian Liturgy

Just as Christianity developed out of Judaism, so too did the worship practices of the early church grow out of Jewish liturgy. The liturgical practices of Judaism had three primary focuses: prayer and sacrifice at the Temple; a daily, weekly, and annual cycle of prayers, blessings, and feasts; and synagogue worship, which centered primarily on teaching and remembrance. Early Christians embraced these Jewish patterns of worship, adding their own practices related to the life and teachings of Jesus, as outlined in the New Testament.

The liturgical practices of the early church recognized the need for both continuity with the old patterns of the Jewish faith and transformation of certain elements in light of their belief in Jesus as the Christ. According to the Book of Acts, the first Christians continued to worship in synagogues on the Sabbath and at the Temple in Jerusalem. They also celebrated the Eucharist, or "the Lord's Supper," on the day of the resurrection, Sunday. After the persecution of Christians began, and followers of Jesus were no longer allowed to meet in synagogues, they established their own order and form of worship. The pattern they developed mirrored the synagogue worship structure—a litany, confession, eulogies and other prayers, readings from sacred scriptures, an address or sermon, and a benediction—but included the uniquely Christian practice of the Eucharist just before the benediction. Christian worship continued in this mode for roughly 1,500 years.

Over time, differences developed between the Eastern and Western branches of Christianity. Later, the Protestant Reformation led to a dramatically different understanding of what Christian worship should be. This gallery explores some of the ways in which these various liturgical traditions draw their inspiration and authority from the text of the Bible.

Eastern Orthodoxy: Worshiping with All Five Senses   [Case 8400]

Worship in the Eastern Orthodox Church follows a pattern very similar to that practiced by the early Christians. The Divine Liturgy, which is celebrated by Orthodox Christians on Sunday morning and on major feast days, consists of two parts. The first—modeled after Jewish liturgical patterns—includes a litany, various other hymns and prayers, readings from the Bible, and a sermon. Readings are scheduled according to the church calendar, with specific passages from the Gospels, Epistles, and Old Testament assigned for each day of the year. Books that contain these readings in order are called lectionaries (Item 8401). The second half of the service is the celebration of Holy Communion.

Case 8400 – Item Diagnostics

8401:	**GOSPEL LECTIONARY IN GREEK**	8403:	**CENSER FOR HOME USE**
	Copied by the scribe Theodore		Brass
	Decorated manuscript on parchment		Greece
	Byzantium		20th century
	Dated 1147/1148 AD in scribal colophon		*Loan courtesy of Deacon Aaron Taylor*
	GC.MS.000455		
8402:	**DIPTYCH ICON, FEATURING THE CHRIST AND ST. ATHANASIUS**	8404:	***KOMBOSCHOINI*** **(PRAYER ROPE)**
	Tempera on wood		Wool
	Greece		Mount Athos (Autonomous Monastic State of the Holy Mountain)
	Mid-20th century		21st century
	Loan courtesy of Deacon Aaron Taylor		*Loan courtesy of Deacon Aaron Taylor*

One of the practices unique to the Orthodox Church is the use of icons (Item 8402). Icons are sacred works of art that depict scenes from the Bible or important figures, like the Christ, the Virgin Mary, and various saints. Icons provide a spiritual connection between the worshiper and the person, time, or place depicted. Because of this, they are often called "windows into heaven." The images are highly symbolic. They are intended to convey theological truths and draw the viewer into contemplation, not to be a realistic illustration of a particular story. In the Orthodox Church, icons are venerated, or paid deep respect, although this respect is ultimately intended for the person depicted in the icon, and not directed at the image itself.

Another common devotional practice is the use of the *komboschoini*, or prayer rope (Item 8404). On each knot, the user prays the Jesus Prayer: "Lord Jesus Christ, Son of God, have mercy on me, a sinner." Prayer ropes are commonly used by Orthodox monks, who are seeking to "pray without ceasing" (1 Thessalonians 5:17, ESV) by repeating this prayer hundreds of times a day. This particular *komboschoini* was made by a monk living on Mount Athos, known to Orthodox as the Holy Mountain.

The liturgical practices of the Orthodox Church engage all five senses in the act of worshiping God. The congregation's sight is engaged by icons and colorful vestments. They listen to the chanting of the prayers and Bible readings, and taste the bread and wine during the Eucharist. Various physical motions like standing, kneeling, praying with a *komboschoini*, and making the sign of the cross employ the sense of touch. Even the sense of smell is engaged through the use of incense (Item 8403), which represents prayers going up to heaven reflecting the words of Psalm 141:2, "Let my prayer be counted as incense before you" (ESV).

"First, Last, and Center": The Psalter in the Russian Orthodox Church   [Case 8500]

For Orthodox Christians, perhaps the most important section of the Bible (after the Gospels) is the Psalter, or the Book of Psalms. St. John Chrysostom, Archbishop of Constantinople in the fourth century AD, said that the Psalms were "first, last, and center" to Christian worship, and this is something that continues to be visibly lived out in the Orthodox Church.

Case 8500 – Item Diagnostics

8501:	PSALTER IN OLD CHURCH SLAVONIC
	Decorated manuscript on parchment
	Serbia
	Late 14th or early 15th century
	Serbia
	GC.MS.000456

In Eastern Orthodoxy, the Psalter is divided into 20 *kathismata*, or divisions, from the word for "sitting," since the congregation typically sits during the reading of the Psalms. These *kathismata* are further divided into three *stases* each, from the word which means to stand, since each *stases* typically ends with the "Glory Be to the Father" prayer, during which the congregation stands. The *kathismata* are read (often chanted) at morning and evening prayer each day, so that the entire Psalter is read each week. During Great Lent, or the period of preparation before Easter, the schedule of readings intensifies, so that the Psalms are completely read through twice in a week. There are a number of other instances where the Psalms are read in the Orthodox tradition. For example, when an Orthodox Christian dies, typically his or her body is moved to the church on the night before burial. Friends and family then keep a vigil through the night, where they read the Psalter continuously over the person's body.

Within Eastern Orthodoxy, there are a number of different regional churches. These churches all hold to the same doctrinal beliefs, but the particular form of the liturgy might vary. One of these regional branches is the Russian Orthodox Church. When Cyril and Methodius traveled as missionaries to Moravia in the ninth century AD, their desire was to plant an independent church that could conduct the liturgy in the local language. Therefore, the Psalter was one of the first books of the Bible they translated in the process creating a literary language now known as Old Church Slavonic (Item 8501).

Ethiopian Orthodox Tewahedo Church   [Case 8600]

Ethiopia traces its Christian heritage to Philip the Evangelist. In Acts 8, Philip baptizes an Ethiopian eunuch who was a high-ranking official in the Ethiopian court. Ethiopic tradition says that the newly baptized eunuch returned home, where he shared the news of what he had learned with others.

Case 8600 – Item Diagnostics

8601:	PSALTER WITH CANTICLES AND WEDDASE MARYAM IN GE'EZ Decorated manuscript on parchment Ethiopia Early 20th century GC.MS.000298	8604:	HAND CROSS, WITH IMAGE OF THE VIRGIN AND CHILD Silver Ethiopia 20th century GC.OBJ.000134
8602:	GOSPELS IN GE'EZ Decorated manuscript on parchment Ethiopia Circa 1400 GC.MS.000146	8605:	TRIPTYCH ICON, FEATURING THE VIRGIN AND CHILD Gondarine School Tempera and gesso on wood Ethiopia 17th century GC.ART.000246.1-.3
8603:	"HORN OF THE LAMB OF GOD" HAND CROSS, WITH IMAGE OF THE CRUCIFIXION Wood Ethiopia 17th century GC.OBJ.000118	8606:	DOUBLE-SIDED PENDANT ICON, FEATURING THE VIRGIN AND CHILD, ST. GEORGE, AND THE CRUCIFIXION Tempera and gesso on wood Ethiopia 17th century GC.ART.000229.1-.3

In the early fourth century AD, Christianity became the official religion of Ethiopia under King Ezana of Aksum. The king was taught Christianity by St. Frumentius, a Greek from Tyre who had been brought to Ethiopia as a child. Ethiopic tradition also credits him with translating the Greek Bible into Ge'ez, which is still the official language of the Ethiopian Orthodox Tewahedo Church (Item 8602). Remaining relatively isolated for several centuries, this church developed distinct liturgical and iconographic traditions. One distinct liturgical practice is the *Weddasé Maryam*, or "Praise of Mary," a collection of seven prayers—one for each day of the week—honoring Mary, the mother of Jesus. These prayers are often attached to the end of Psalters, or books containing the Psalms and the Canticles (Item 8601).

Another liturgical practice of Ethiopic Christianity is the display of crosses and icons on holy days and during public processions. The two hand crosses shown in this case would have been carried by priests during a public procession and used to give a blessing (Items 8603, 8604). The crosses bear scenes regularly depicted in Ethiopian iconography: an image of Jesus sitting on his mother Mary's lap, known as the "Virgin and Child," and an image of the crucifixion. Similar imagery can be seen on the two icons in this case (Items 8605, 8606).

Today, the Ethiopian Orthodox Tewahedo Church belongs to the communion of Oriental Orthodox Churches, which separated from the Eastern Orthodox Church in the fifth century AD. They are separate, therefore, from churches like the Greek or Russian Orthodox.

Liturgical Significance Explored

Biblical Understanding of Communion

Despite drawing from the same sacred text, Christian denominations come to very different conclusions about the Bible's meaning and its impact on worship practices. This is most evident, perhaps, in the act of communion. Some Christian denominations view it as a sacrament in which Christ is physically present, others believe that

Christ is spiritually present as a special action of the Holy Spirit, and others think of it as a purely symbolic memorial of Christ's redemptive sacrifice and death. In all cases, adherents point to the Bible to support their particular understanding.

Altar Area – Item Diagnostics

Large Communion Table
Oak
United States
19th century
GC.FUR.000119

The practice of communion in many Protestant churches is memorial. In the gospel accounts of Jesus' last meal with his disciples, he broke bread and gave it to them saying, "This is my body, which is given for you. Do this ***in remembrance*** of me" (Luke 22:19, ESV; emphasis added). By reenacting this meal, memorialists have an opportunity to reflect on the sacrificial nature of the crucifixion. In this understanding of communion, the bread and wine are purely symbolic since Jesus himself administered the celebration with the elements.

Many Christian denominations, on the other hand, believe that once the bread and wine of communion are consecrated by the priest, they become the body and blood of Christ, and bestow grace upon those who receive them. There are many different views of what precisely it means for the bread and wine to "become" the body and blood of Christ, however. These Christians also draw upon Jesus' words at the Last Supper—"***This is my body***, which is given for you. ***Do this*** in remembrance of me" (Luke 22:19, ESV; emphasis added)—for support, but focus on different parts of the verse. This sacramental understanding of the Eucharist also draws from John 6, when Jesus says,

> *If anyone eats of this bread, he will live forever. And the bread that I will give for the life of the world is my flesh… Truly, truly, I say to you, unless you eat the flesh of the Son of Man and drink his blood, you have no life in you.* (John 6:51–53, ESV)

Even the method of taking communion varies widely among Christians. Some traditions have people go up to the altar to receive communion, where they all drink out of the same cup, called a chalice. This emphasizes an understanding of communion as a communal experience, shared not only with others taking communion that day, but also with all Christians throughout history. In other traditions, the bread and wine (often grape juice) is distributed individually, emphasizing an understanding of communion first as a moment between the individual and God, second between the individual and their local church body, and third between the individual and the greater body of believers around the world. There are several variations of these two forms.

The Catholic Church and Its Liturgy   [Case 8700]

Just as the liturgical practices of the early Christians found their Eastern expression in the Orthodox Church, so too has the Catholic Church preserved many of their basic forms in the West. Like the Orthodox Divine Liturgy, Catholic Mass is made up of two sections: the Liturgy of the Word—which includes prayers, the creed, readings from the Bible, and a sermon—and the Liturgy of the Eucharist. Everything the priest needs to conduct the service, from prayers and readings to instructions and sometimes even musical notation, is written in the missal (Item 8701).

Catholics also use a lectionary to follow a set order of readings for use throughout the church year (Item 8703). Unlike the Eastern Orthodox lectionary, the Western lectionary is arranged according to a three-year cycle, focusing on a different Synoptic Gospel (Matthew, Mark, or Luke) each year.

Because of the belief that Christ is physically present in the bread consecrated during communion, many Catholics participate in a service called Benediction of the Blessed Sacrament. During a Benediction service, the consecrated host is placed on display in a monstrance (Item 8702). A period of adoration follows, during which the congregation sings hymns and prays. Finally, the priest uses the monstrance to make the sign of blessing over the congregation. (For more information on varying Christian beliefs about communion, see the "Liturgical Significance Explored" area at the front of this gallery.)

Another devotional practice commonly observed by Catholics is praying the rosary (Item 8704). Like the Greek Orthodox *komboschoini* (see case 8400), rosary beads are used to focus the mind during prayer. The beads are used to count the prayers said during the rosary, including the Lord's Prayer, the Hail Mary, and the Glory Be to the Father prayers. While saying these prayers, the person praying the rosary also meditates on a set of five "mysteries," or events in the life of Mary and Jesus. These are:

- "The Joyful Mysteries," like the annunciation, the nativity, and Jesus' presentation at the Temple
- "The Sorrowful Mysteries," which focus on the death and passion of Jesus
- "The Glorious Mysteries," such as the resurrection, the ascension, and the coming of the Holy Spirit on Pentecost
- "The Luminous Mysteries," including Jesus' baptism, the miracle at the wedding feast in Cana, and the transfiguration

Case 8700 – Item Diagnostics

8701:	**MISSAL IN LATIN, WITH MUSICAL NOTATION** Illuminated manuscript on parchment Paris or Normandy Circa 1320–1330 GC.MS.000841	8703:	**GOSPEL LECTIONARY OF CISTERCIAN USE, IN LATIN** Illuminated manuscript on parchment Northwest Italy, possibly for Morimondo Abbey Circa 1200–1225 GC.MS.000482
8702:	**MONSTRANCE WITH LUNA** Brass 21st century GC.EP.000010.1-.2	8704:	**ROSARY** Connemara marble Ireland Late 20th century *On loan from a Private Collection*

Anglicanism: The *Via Media*   [Case 8800]

With King Henry VIII's break from Rome and the English Reformation came the birth of a new denomination, Anglicanism. Anglicanism—also known as the Church of England, the Episcopal Church, or other names depending on where in the world you are—embraced some of the theological reforms of the Protestant Reformation, while still keeping many of the Catholic traditions and hierarchy and understandings. For this reason, it has been called the *via media*, or "the middle way," between Protestantism and Catholicism.

Worship in the Anglican Church is outlined in the Book of Common Prayer (Items 8801, 8803). The book, written by Archbishop of Canterbury Thomas Cramner, was first published in 1549. It outlines the order of service for morning and evening prayer, the Great Litany, Holy Communion, and numerous other services that are celebrated throughout the course of the church year. These services were very similar to their Catholic predecessors; what was radically different was the Book of Common Prayer itself. This book recorded everything that was going to be said in a service—both by the priests and by the laity—in plain English, a very Protestant departure from the Catholic missal, which was used by the priest alone and recited in Latin.

Case 8800 – Item Diagnostics

8801:	**BOOK OF COMMON PRAYER**
	Printed by Robert Barker
	Ink on paper
	London, England
	1605
	GC.PBK.002284
8802:	**EUCHARISTIC VEIL, CORPORAL, AND BURSE**
	Velvet and damask
	Poland
	21st century
	Loan courtesy of Father H. Jay Atwood
8803:	**BOOK OF COMMON PRAYER, WITH LITURGY FOR THE GUN POWDER PLOT**
	Printed by William Pearson
	Ink and pigment on paper
	London, England
	1711
	GC.PBK.000129

As with the Catholic and Orthodox denominations, the central element of worship in the Anglican Church is the celebration of Holy Communion. Because the consecrated elements of the Eucharist are so sacred, they are shrouded by a decorative veil (Item 8802), much like practice of covering the Torah in Judaism. In England in the Late Middle Ages, only the priests received communion regularly. The rest of the congregation was only allowed to receive communion once a year, on Easter. One of the reforms Cranmer enacted was to encourage Anglican priests to administer communion to their congregations weekly—and to prohibit priests from ever taking communion alone. The Book of Common Prayer on the left (Item 8801) is open to the words of consecration, which come from 1 Corinthians 11:23-25.

The Book of Common Prayer has undergone numerous editorial revisions since it was first printed. Occasionally entirely new services are added, as with Item 8803, which contains a service for the anniversary of the Gunpowder Plot of 1605, when an attempt to overthrow the British government was successfully prevented.

The Bible and Protestant Worship   [Case 8900]

Protestants largely adhere to a form of "low church," which emphasizes simplicity and individualism in worship, in contrast to the formalities and rituals of more "high church" traditions. This shift can be traced back to the Protestant Reformation. Martin Luther disagreed with the Roman Catholic Church on theological principles, and while he disagreed with certain rituals of the church, he did not reject them all. He believed that many of the worship traditions were acceptable, as long as they were not expressly forbidden in the Bible. Huldrych Zwingli, a contemporary of Luther, did not think Luther went far enough, however. Zwingli rejected all rituals that were not specifically mentioned in the Bible (mostly the New Testament). The degree of simplicity progressed amongst groups of Protestants, eventually birthing minimalist liturgical movements such as the Puritans, Quakers, Anabaptists, Mennonites, and the Amish.

Because every Protestant denomination determines its own views on theology and liturgy, usually without any outside governing authority, Protestant worship can look quite different from church to church. Typically, every church has a different style, order of service, type of music, and view on things like modesty, morality, and family. In fact, worship in a Protestant church need not occur within the walls of a building at all, and it is not uncommon for families to conduct worship at home (Item 8905). One thing that is almost universal about worship among Protestants, however, is that the sermon replaced the Eucharist as the central moment in the service. Eventually, people flocked to listen to sermons from popular evangelists, like John Wesley, George Whitefield, Billy Graham, and Billy Sunday (Item 8906).

One thing most Protestant denominations have in common, though, is congregational music. Groups of songs would be compiled together in hymnbooks for use during the service (Items 8901, 8902, 8903, 8904). As Protestants diversified, different hymnbooks emerged specific to a particular denomination. Modern technology gives churches the ability to project words onto a screen, thus making the use of hymnbooks less common and highlighting the difference between a "high church" adherence to tradition and a "low church" embrace of innovation and change.

Case 8900 – Item Diagnostics

8901:	ISAAC WATTS, *THE PSALMS OF DAVID: IMITATED IN THE LANGUAGE OF THE NEW TESTAMENT...* Ink on paper London, England 1719 GC.BIB.002436	8904:	IRA SANKEY, *GOSPEL HYMNS AND SACRED SONGS* Ink on paper England Circa 1890 GC.PBK.000618
8902:	*LITURGY AND HYMNS FOR USE OF PROTESTANT CHURCH OF THE UNITED BRETHREN* Ink on paper United States 1861 GC.PBK.002283	8905:	*FAMILY BIBLE* Ink on paper Likely England 19th century GC.BIB.003077
8903:	JOHN NEWTON, *OLNEY HYMNS* Ink on paper Likely England 1779 GC.PBK.000663	8906:	BILLY SUNDAY, *PERSONAL JOURNAL WITH SERMON NOTES* Ink on paper United States Early 20th century GC.MS.000769

Adornment of and Art about the Bible

In the history of art, the Bible has been the source of seemingly endless artistic inspiration. For all the impact that the Bible has had on art, however, the reverse is also true. Art has made the content of the Bible relatable, accessible, debatable, and inspirational.

For hundreds of years, Christians have relied on images to convey the stories of the Bible and their deeper meanings to people who could not read them for themselves, using a variety of methods, such as painting, frescos, sculpture, and stained glass. As more people learned to read, pictures were used to adorn the Bible and to help people connect with the stories on a deeper, more personal, level.

Today, art is overwhelmingly absent from adult Bibles, left only to children's books and Sunday school classrooms. For the majority of the history of Christianity, however, exactly the opposite was true. The most important Bibles were the ones that were extensively decorated, both inside and out.

This room contains beautifully illuminated manuscripts from the Middle Ages, intricately engraved Bibles from the Renaissance, fore-edge painted Bibles from the Victorian era, and an array of spectacular bindings. The process of illustrating and adorning the Bible is a challenge that has attracted many of the most famous artists throughout history. Though the style of the art changes depending on the time and place in which it was made, the scenes depicted—and the themes conveyed—remain familiar.

Beautiful Devotion: The Art of Illumination   [Case 9000]

Case 9000 – Item Diagnostics

9001:	**PSALTER WITH CANTICLES AND WEDDASE MARYAM**
	Illuminated manuscript on parchment
	Ethiopia
	19th century
	GC.MS.000299
9002:	**BOOK OF HOURS, USE OF TOURNAI**
	NEO-GOTHIC ILLUMINATIONS BY THE SPANISH FORGER
	Illuminated manuscript on parchment
	France
	1450, with additions of late 19th–early 20th century
	GC.MS.000167
9003:	**ARMENIAN PSALTER, FEATURING A FULL-PAGE MINIATURE OF KING DAVID WITH DECORATIVE HEADPIECE ON FACING PAGE**
	Signed by the Painter Markos "The Illuminator"
	Illuminated manuscript on parchment
	Constantinople, Turkey
	1659
	GC.MS.000147
9004:	**BOOK OF HOURS, USE OF SALISBURY**
	GIFT OF HENRY VIII TO HIS COUSIN, INDICATED BY AN INSCRIPTION IN THE KING'S HAND
	Printed by Simon Vostre
	Printed book on parchment with hand-illuminations
	Paris, France
	1512
	GC.PBK.002282
9005:	**BOOK OF HOURS, USE OF ROME, FEATURING MINIATURE OF THE FLIGHT TO EGYPT**
	Illuminated manuscript on parchment
	Burgundy, France
	Late 15th century
	GC.MS.000152

Medieval manuscripts are known for their elaborately decorated borders and theologically rich illustrations, called "illuminations." The term comes from the Latin word *illuminare*—"to light up or to illuminate." Most illuminations include gold gilding, which literally lights up the page. They also serve to "illuminate," or make clear with pictures, the meaning of the text.

During the Middle Ages, this work was done by an "illuminator." Adding illuminations to a manuscript was an expensive undertaking, and people often used illumination to convey their wealth or status. Even after the birth of printing, some patrons still chose to have their books illuminated by hand, as is the case with a Book of Hours given as a gift by King Henry VIII (Item 9004). In the late nineteenth century, one industrious forger even began adding his own illuminations to manuscripts, passing them off as genuine, in an attempt to capitalize on the renewed interest in the Middle Ages (Item 9002). Other cultures continue to decorate their sacred texts by hand (Item 9001).

This case contains illuminated books of two distinct types, the Psalter and the Book of Hours. Psalters (Items 9001, 9003) contain the biblical book of Psalms, often incorporating other devotional material as well. These small devotional books were commonly commissioned and used by the wealthy, thus the imagery can be quite personal and revealing about its owner.

In the Late Middle Ages, the Psalter gave way to the Book of Hours as the most popular type of book used for personal devotion. The Book of Hours (Items 9002, 9004, 9005) contains prayers and readings similarly arranged according to the canonical hours, or the times during the day set aside for prayer. These prayers were often accompanied by cycles of meditations on the life of Christ or the life of Mary. These cycles were marked out by full-page miniatures depicting the scenes that were to be contemplated.

Preaching with Pictures: Illustrations as Teaching Aids   [Case 9100]

This case contains a manuscript copy of the *Speculum Humanae Salvationis*, or the *Mirror of Human Salvation*, a popular work of theology that circulated during the Late Medieval Period (Item 9101). It features over

Case 9100 – Item Diagnostics

9101:	**MIRROR OF HUMAN SALVATION**
	Pen-and-ink drawings by "Magister Konrad"
	Decorated manuscript on parchment
	Tyrol, Austria
	Circa 1370
	GC.MS.000321

192 pen-and-ink illuminations made by Magister Konrad, a famous Austrian illuminator. Designed to help less-educated preachers and members of the laity better understand the Bible, the text relies primarily on images to convey places where events in the Old Testament and other texts foreshadow, or point toward, events in the New Testament. This type of interpretation is known as a typological interpretation of the Bible.

The manuscript is open to two facing pages. Starting on the far left, you see an image of the Last Supper, or the last meal Jesus shared with his disciples, which is narrated in Matthew 26, Mark 14, Luke 22, and John 13. Set alongside this New Testament story are three Old Testament parallels: the miracle of manna (Exodus 16:14–17), the Passover (Exodus 18), and Melchizedek giving Abraham bread and wine (Genesis 14:18–20).

Printed Adornment: Engravings of the Renaissance   [Case 9200]

The evolution of printing, which allowed for the mass production of books, is one of the most influential movements in history. As with the manuscripts they replaced, printed books were often decorated with pictures, providing that much needed connection between the reader and the text. The early stages of printed images began with woodblocks, which eventually led to metal etching and lithography.

The most influential engraver of the fifteenth and sixteenth centuries was Albrecht Dürer (1471–1528). His attention to detail, knowledge of perspective, mathematical proportions, and understanding of the natural world made him an unparalleled artist of his day. His works were so popular that people added his prints to books that did not contain images, like the image of Christ's *Agony in the Garden* pasted into the manuscript shown in this case (Item 9201)

Case 9200 – Item Diagnostics

9201:	**GEORGE SCHERER, *THE MYSTERIES OF THE PASSION OF OUR LORD JESUS CHRIST*, FEATURING ENGRAVINGS BY ALBRECHT DÜRER**
	Open to a print of the *Agony in the Garden*
	Manuscript on parchment and paper
	Vienna, Austria
	1591
	GC.MS.000153

9202:	**NICOLAUS JOHANNES VISSCHER, *BIBLICAL THEATRE, THAT IS, THE SACRED HISTORIES OF THE OLD AND NEW TESTAMENTS PORTRAYED USING COPPER ENGRAVINGS***
	Open to a print of priests carrying the Ark of the Covenant through the River Jordan
	Ink on paper
	Amsterdam, Holland
	1650
	GC.PBK.000169.1

9203:	***THE MOST REMARKABLE HISTORIES OF THE OLD AND NEW TESTAMENT***
	Open to a print of Zacchaeus
	Copper Engravings by Jean Luyken, Jean Covens and Cornielle Mortier
	Ink on paper
	Amsterdam, Holland
	1732
	GC.PBK.000364

Perhaps the best known of Dürer's biblical engravings is that of the *Four Horsemen of the Apocalypse*. It is characteristic of Dürer's highly dramatic compositions, emphasizing a theatrical moment of imminent action. This theatricality continued as later artists of the seventeenth century created engravings with a similar flare for the dramatic (Items 9202, 9203).

Illustrations of Purpose: Themes Enhanced by Engravings   [Case 9300]

The eighteenth and nineteenth centuries saw the rapid rise of "thematic Bibles," or Bibles designed with a specific group in mind. While this was not a new concept, it was expanded to include more diverse options. The number of people who owned and read the Bible was increasing, and with it the variety of interests people were bringing to the text.

Case 9300 – Item Diagnostics

9301:	**DEVOTIONAL FAMILY BIBLE WITH ILLUSTRATIONS** Open to a print of Esther pleading for her people before the king Ink on paper London, England Circa 1850 GC.BIB.000451
9302:	**THE NEW TESTAMENT, IN DUTCH** Open to a large, fold-out map Ink on paper Amsterdam, Holland 1720 GC.BIB.000690
9303:	**JACOB SCHEUCHZER, *PHYSICA SACRA* (SCIENTIFIC COMMENTARY ON THE BIBLE), VOLUME I** Printed by Christian Ulrich Wagner Ink on paper Augsburg, Germany 1731 GC.BIB.003840.1

One such group was that of the naturalist, a person interested in studying natural history. A man named Jakob Scheuchzer set out to create a Bible that used the elements in the natural world to explain the Bible's supernatural themes (Item 9303). It is full of beautiful copper engravings depicting plants, animals, and other natural things. This *Physica Sacra* became the foremost authority on such things, and it is still referenced today.

The most common of such interest groups were, and still are, the family and the individual researcher. Large, devotional family Bibles included many beautiful illustrations, and many considered them a family treasure, using them to keep records of births, deaths, marriages, and the like (Item 9301). At the same time, personal study Bibles were created to include commentaries, maps, indexes, and notes (Item 9302). Both the study Bible and the family Bible continue to be the most common thematic Bibles today.

Painting the Page: Fore-Edge Painting   [Case 9400]

The fore-edge is the side of a book opposite the spine, where the pages are exposed. In the Middle Ages, this—and not the spine—was often used to record a book's title or shelfmark. There is evidence that as early as the tenth century people began to utilize this often overlooked area of the book for decoration. The earliest examples are mostly patterns and designs, but as the centuries passed, the art form began to expand into full scenes. The scenes depicted often emulate what the text was about, but not always. Sometimes the artwork on the fore-edge was simply a way to make the book more beautiful. Take, for instance, the Bibles in this case. Some of them depict biblical scenes (Items 9401, 9405, 9406), one depicts a religious location (Item 9403), and the others depict locations that might have had some personal meaning for the owner (Items 9402, 9404).

There are a few different types of fore-edge painting. The earliest type can be seen when the book is completely closed. Other types of fore-edge painting are only seen when the pages are fanned out slightly, as shown here. Some books may have multiple scenes painted on a single fore-edge. One may be on the direct edge, another fanned out facing the front, and a third fanned out facing the back.

Case 9400 – Item Diagnostics

9401:	**BIBLE WITH FORE-EDGE PAINTING OF THE LORD'S SUPPER** Printed by British and Foreign Bible Society Ink and pigment on paper London, England 1891 GC.BIB.000814	9404:	**BIBLE WITH FORE-EDGE PAINTING OF BEDDINGTON PARK, SURREY** Painted by Helen R. Haywood Ink and pigment on paper London, England Circa 1820 GC.BIB.000583
9402:	**BIBLE WITH FORE-EDGE PAINTING OF MISSISSIPPI STEAMBOATS** Painted by Martin Frost Printed by Oxford University Press Ink and pigment on paper Oxford, England 1854 GC.BIB.000343	9405:	**BIBLE WITH FORE-EDGE PAINTING OF THE CRUCIFIXION** Printed by Samuel Collingworth and Co. Ink and pigment on paper Oxford, England 1826 GC.BIB.000828
9403:	**BOOK OF COMMON PRAYER WITH FORE-EDGE PAINTING OF ST. PAUL'S CATHEDRAL** Painted by Martin Frost Ink and pigment on paper London, England 1739 GC.PBK.000235	9406:	**BIBLE WITH FORE-EDGE PAINTING OF ABRAHAM AND LOT LEAVING UR** Painted by John T. Beer Printed by Robert Barker London, England 1637 GC.BIB.000607

Spectacular Bindings: Covered with Beauty   [Case 9500]

A book's cover is, first and foremost, functional, but it can also be beautiful. The Bibles and religious texts in this case are exquisite examples of this very concept. The binding is an outward display symbolizing the importance of the book or the owner. One instance of this is the large Bible covered in mother of pearl with an accompanying box (Item 9501). The Palestinian leader Yasser Arafat gave this fine set to a European diplomat.

Silver bindings were a popular choice for their luminescence and variation (Items 9502, 9504, 9506). The silver could be molded, carved, spun, or hammered into the desired design. Jewish Bibles were often decorated in fine silver craftsmanship (Item 9504). This work by Jewish silversmiths can also be seen on coverings and accessories for the Torah. In Jewish tradition, the Torah is not to be illuminated or illustrated in any way. The text is considered too sacred. The coverings for the Torah, however, were a different story. In this tradition, the covering is meant to honor the text.

The most popular binding material is leather. Artisans throughout history have created beautiful covers with stamped, embossed, gilded, painted, and embellished leather (Items 9507, 9508, 9509, 9511). Wood was also used for its ability to be carved and shaped. Occasionally more unique materials are employed, like embroidered fabric (Item 9503) and amber (Item 9510). This amber-covered Bible is one of only three unique editions made by German amber workers in 1909, each featuring a different design. This is believed to be the only one still surviving.

Case 9500 – Item Diagnostics

9501:	**KING JAMES BIBLE WITH MOTHER OF PEARL INLAY ON BINDING IN MOTHER OF PEARL BOX** Gift of Yasser Arafat to a European Leader Mother of pearl Palestine 20th century GC.BIB.002929, GC.OBJ.000371.1-.2	**9507:**	**BIBLE WITH STAMPED LEATHER BINDING** Leather London, England 1653 GC.BIB.000977.2
9502:	**GOSPELS IN GREEK, WITH SILVER COVER** Silver Athens, Greece 1899 GC.BIB.001624	**9508:**	**PSALMS, PROVERBS, ECCLESIASTES, WISDOM, AND ECCLESIASTICUS, WITH STAMPED LEATHER BINDING** Printed by J. and D. Elizevier Ink on paper; leather Leiden, Germany; France (binding) 1653; 18th century (binding) GC.BIB.001083
9503:	**BOOK OF PSALMS, BOUND WITH THE NEW TESTAMENT IN "DOS-Á-DOS" FORMAT (TWO WORKS BOUND BACK TO BACK)** Embroidered fabric binding London, England 1633 GC.BIB.002472	**9509:**	**BOOK OF COMMON PRAYER, WITH STAMPED LEATHER BINDING** Leather Paris, France 1791 GC.BIB.001357
9504:	**HEBREW BIBLE WITH SILVER COVER** Silver Date Unknown GC.BIB.002927	**9510:**	**GERMAN BIBLE, FEATURING AN AMBER COVER** Leather and amber Germany 1909–1969 GC.BIB.002928
9505:	**LITANY FROM BOOK OF COMMON PRAYER, FOR THE USE OF THE CHURCH OF ALL SAINTS, WITH CARVED WOODEN BOARD COVER** Wood Cheltenham, England Date Unknown GC.MS.000334	**9511:**	**PHILIPP MELANCHTHON, *COLLECTION OF CHRISTIAN DOCTRINE*, FEATURING MARTIN LUTHER ON FRONT COVER** Leather Leipzig, Germany 1565 GC.PBK.000404
9506:	**BOOK OF COMMON PRAYER WITH SILVER COVER** Silver London, England Date Unknown GC.PBK.000631		

Contemporary Art and the Bible: Freud, Dali, and Moses   [Case 9600]

Here is an intriguing example of how modern philosophy, religious ideas, and modern art merge. The spectacular, metal-molded, over-sized cover in this case was created by the twentieth-century Spanish, surrealist artist Salvador Dali (Item 9601). It contains ten lithographs, a type of printing where the images is etched into a waxy surface applied over a piece of metal.

In these lithographs, Dali was illustrating *Moses and Monotheism*, written by the early twentieth-century psychologist Sigmund Freud. In this work, Freud argues that Moses was actually an Egyptian, not Hebrew. Attempting to convey Freud's thesis, Dali's lithograph cover—a bas-relief sculpture cast from a wax mold—depicts Moses in the eye of Horus.

The lithograph on display, entitled *The Dream of Moses*, shows Moses laying asleep and dreaming of Egyptian landmarks such as the pyramids and a sphinx (Item 9602). In the center of the work is a bull, perhaps representing the Egyptian god Hathor or Apis; it may also be foreshadowing the golden calf. To Dali, the bull represents the monotheistic god. He emphasizes the point by depicting a Roman Catholic bishop in a miter approaching the animal. A black angel sits atop some ruins, watching the spectacle.

Case 9600 – Item Diagnostics

9601:	SALVADOR DALI, MOLDED COVER DEPICTING MOSES IN THE EYE OF HORUS Containing ten original color prints on *Moses and Monotheism* by Sigmund Freud Metal and velvet Figueres, Spain 1975 GC.ART.000278.37	9602:	SALVADOR DALI, "THE DREAM OF MOSES" One of ten original color prints on *Moses and Monotheism* by Sigmund Freud Lithograph engraving on sheepskin Figueres, Spain 1975 GC.ART.000278.10

Biblical Art in Sacred Spaces: The Beauty and Function of Stained Glass   [Case 9700]

It was once thought that stained glass was an exclusively Christian medium. Relatively recent discoveries, however, have uncovered mosaic bits of glass used in decorative arts from as early as the Roman period. There is also evidence of use by Arabian artisans, using geometric designs to stay true to their stance on non-figural art. By the tenth century, artists in northern Europe began to use lead reinforcements around the glass pieces, since they have weather that is more inclement and needed a strong material to hold the windows together. Despite its use beyond the Christian realm, stained glass can be found in many churches, usually featuring biblical subjects. The popularity of this art form reached its height during the Gothic period, which ran from roughly the twelfth through the sixteenth centuries, when innovations in construction allowed for larger windows. The images were intricate in execution and dense with symbolism, often becoming a teaching tool to supplement reading the text of the Bible. This magnificent style of art continues to be used today.

Case 9700 – Item Diagnostics

9701:	"SAINT LUKE AND SAINT JOHN," WINDOW IN TWO PANELS Designed by Louis Comfort Tiffany and Tiffany Studios Stained glass New York, New York 1905 *Window formerly located in the behind the altar at the Episcopal Church of the Epiphany, Orange, New Jersey* GC.ART.001168.1-.2

The two stained glass windows on display (Item 9701), depicting the apostles Luke and John, are from the Church of the Epiphany in Orange, New Jersey. They are part of a larger set of windows that include the other two evangelists, Matthew and Mark, and a scene depicting Jesus on the morning of the resurrection. All of the windows were designed and created by the famous Tiffany Studios of New York City.

Artistic Techniques Explored

The Art of Stained Glass and the Innovations of Louis Comfort Tiffany

Louis Comfort Tiffany (ca. 1848–1933) was an artist and interior designer in New York City. He became fascinated with stained glass after a visit to the Victoria and Albert Museum in London, prompting him to found Tiffany Studios in 1902. He developed many innovative techniques in glass production that would immortalize his name in the industry. The production of his stained glass windows and lampshades became widely popular in the first few decades of the twentieth century. This popularity lasted until around 1930, when it began to be considered old-fashioned and out of style. It saw a resurgence of popularity in the late 1970s that continues.

Some glass techniques created by Tiffany, and seen in the windows on display, are:

Favrile Glass

A method of infusing molten glass with a variety of colors (often shimmering, opalescent colors) and swirling them around to gain the desired implied texture.

Mottled Glass

A favorite among modern abstract artists, this speckled, implied texture was often used to give the illusion of leaves in the trees, and created by using isolated heating methods combined with a crystalline growth.

Drapery Glass

A technique that replicated and exaggerated imperfections in the glass, manipulating the molten glass similar to a blown-glass artist. The result was real folds and curves creating cast shadows, making the glass look like real drapery.

Layered Glass

The windows seen here are up to four layers thick in some places, creating different dynamics depending on the amounts of light shining through. This can be seen in the radiance of the saint's faces, which is a single pane of glass, and contrasted with some of the darker areas that are multi-layered. In a way, Tiffany was a painter with glass and light, manipulating the media, both natural and created.

"The Battle Hymn of the Republic"

During the Civil War, Union and Confederate soldiers sang numerous anthems while marching to battle. One such song—a favorite of Union soldiers and the bane of the Confederates—was Julia Ward Howe's "Battle Hymn of the Republic." Filled with language and imagery from the Bible, it has developed into an American icon.

Julia Ward Howe first penned the "Battle Hymn" lyrics in the early morning hours of November 19, 1861, at the Willard Hotel in Washington, DC. The previous day she had joined a large group of Union soldiers in singing various popular songs, including "John Brown's Body." James Freemen Clarke, a minister who accompanied Howe to the capital, suggested that she "write some good words for that stirring tune." She did so less than twenty-four hours later, eventually publishing the song in *The Atlantic Monthly* in February 1862.

From its humble beginnings, the "Battle Hymn" spread throughout the Union troops during the Civil War, all the way to President Abraham Lincoln. On February 2, 1864, during a performance in the hall of the House of Representatives, Lincoln was seen tearing up. When the song concluded, Lincoln yelled with tears in his eyes, "Sing it again!" The following year, it was sung at his memorial service in Chicago, IL.

Forged amidst turmoil, "the song that marches on" continues to provide the words for the United States during difficult times. From the Spanish-American War in 1898 to the events of September 11, 2001, the "Battle Hymn of the Republic" has been sung to uplift and empower a weary nation. Its fame has spread, and it has been performed at St. Paul's Cathedral in London several times: on April 20, 1917, to celebrate America entering WWI; again during the state funeral of Prime Minister Winston Churchill in 1965 (by his request); and during a 9/11 memorial service on September 14, 2001.

Abraham Lincoln and the Abolition of Slavery in America   [Case 9800]

Abraham Lincoln was elected President of the United States on November 6, 1860, and inaugurated on March 4, 1861. Between Lincoln's election and inauguration, seven southern states formally seceded to create the "Confederate States of America." Lincoln's economic policies and his outspoken stance against the expansion of slavery received strong opposition from southern states. Four more states seceded shortly after Lincoln's inauguration. For Lincoln, it was imperative that the country remain united, but not at the expense of the country's morality.

Case 9800 – Item Diagnostics

9801:	**SLAVERY BILL OF SALE** *"For… eight hundred dollars… a negro girl Mary Jane… aged sixteen… a slave for life…"* Ink on paper United States December 9, 1854 *Document courtesy of Dr. Ralph Blair*	9803:	**LINCOLN'S INAUGURAL BIBLE, FACSIMILE** Ink on paper United States March 4, 1861 GC.BIB.001570
9802:	**BUST OF ABRAHAM LINCOLN** Metal United States 20th century GC.STA.000153	9804:	**PORTRAIT OF ABRAHAM LINCOLN WITH SIGNATURE, REPRINT** Photographed by Alexander Hesler Reprint on paper Chicago, Illinois 1857; 20th century reprint GC.ART.000418

Like many others of his day, Lincoln thought it was clearly wrong for human beings to be forced into a life of slavery, where they were bought and sold like property (Item 9801). During a speech in 1864, Lincoln said:

"I am naturally anti-slavery. If slavery is not wrong, nothing is wrong. I cannot remember when I did not so think and feel."

His moral understanding was shared by numerous Americans, not least Julia Ward Howe, whom he met briefly in Washington, DC, just days before she penned the first draft of the famous song, "The Battle Hymn of the Republic." Howe later wrote that she was struck by "the sad expression of Mr. Lincoln's deep blue eyes."

Case 9900 – Item Diagnostics

9901:	CABINET PHOTOGRAPH, SIGNED BY JULIA WARD HOWE Paper Boston, Massachusetts 1902 GC.PHO.000203
9902:	ENGRAVING OF JULIA WARD HOWE, PORTRAIT SERIES NO. 279 FROM *THE BOOK NEWS MONTHLY*, SIGNED Paper United States December 1909 GC.ART.000157
9903:	HANDWRITTEN LETTER FROM JULIA WARD HOWE TO AUTHOR EDGAR FAWCETT *"I must thank you too for that humane thirst of your heart which suggested to you the woes of poor mothers in this city…"* Ink on paper Boston, Massachusetts February 5, 1889 GC.PPR.001220
9904:	HANDWRITTEN LETTER FROM JULIA WARD HOWE TO A FRIEND, IN WHICH SHE DISCUSSES THE WOMEN'S CLUB AND OFFERS ENCOURAGEMENT Ink on paper United States September 4, 1903 GC.PPR.001221
9905:	JULIA WARD HOWE, "RECOLLECTION OF THE ANTISLAVERY STRUGGLE," ARTICLE FOR *THE COSMOPOLITAN* MAGAZINE Ink on paper New York, New York 1889 GC.PPR.010171.1-.5

Lincoln was outspoken on his stance against slavery, often discussing it in his speeches and letters. Not everyone agreed. He counter-balanced this divisive stance by emphasizing the importance of a unified nation. In a speech two years before his election and the start of the Civil War, Lincoln cited the Bible to reinforce his point:

A house divided against itself cannot stand. [Mark 3:25] I believe this government cannot endure permanently half-slave and half-free. I do not expect the Union to be dissolved—I do not expect the house to fall—but I do expect it will cease to be divided.

Slavery was not the exclusive cause of the Civil War, but it was a sizeable wedge that served to divide the country. Lincoln dedicated his presidency, and ultimately his life, to removing the ideologies that prevented America from consisting of *United* States.

In Lincoln's inaugural address, he expressed the importance of a unified nation being achieved without unnecessary aggression. Nevertheless, little more than a month after Lincoln was sworn in as president (Item 9803), the Confederacy launched an attack on Fort Sumter, an important Union fort in South Carolina, and set the Civil War in motion.

Julia Ward Howe: Abolitionist, Songwriter, and Social Activist [Case 9900]

The author of the "Battle Hymn of the Republic"—Julia Ward Howe (pictured in Items 9901, 9902)—had many talents, and contributed to society in ways that can still be seen today. Her "Battle Hymn" has solidified itself within American culture, becoming a favorite of important American figures like Abraham Lincoln, Theodore Roosevelt, and Martin Luther King Jr., but the song's renown has often overshadowed the person who fought for women's rights, the abolition of slavery, and peace.

Julia Ward Howe was born into a respectable family in New York City, on May 27, 1819. Her father, Samuel Ward, was a prominent banker who became highly religious when his wife Julia died shortly after the birth of their seventh child. She was twenty-seven. Their oldest daughter, also named Julia, absorbed many of the family responsibilities, and soon became deeply religious as well. She read the Bible thoroughly and even slept with it under her pillow as a child. She enjoyed reading and education of all sorts, studying French, German, Italian, Latin, mathematics, and singing. Her intellectual abilities were impressive, and she utilized them in multiple contexts throughout her life.

Howe used her writing skills to address the abolition of slavery (Item 9905), women's suffrage, and pacifism. In 1870, less than a decade after she first drafted the "Battle Hymn," Howe wrote the "Appeal to Womanhood throughout the World," calling on women to promote global peace. She attempted to initiate a women's international convention to take place in London to discuss world peace, but it never materialized. She later planned the Mother's Day of Peace—a forerunner to Mother's Day—which was held in eighteen American cities on June 2, 1873. Over the course of her life she contributed much of her efforts to the rights of women. Even in her later years, she maintained a chaotic schedule of speaking engagements on topics of women's suffrage, world peace, and anti-prostitution.

Her sentiments for the marginalized people of society were exhibited in both the public and private eye. From the "Battle Hymn" and its abolitionist roots, to her many articles and speeches on the issues of women's suffrage and world peace, her concern for equality was clear. But her consistency in thought is demonstrated in her personal letters, where she still recognized the unappreciated (Item 9103) and discussed the needs of the needy (Item 9104). Julia Ward Howe was a person of integrity, and through her many pursuits she has left a lasting impact on society.

The Battle Hymn's Cultural Impact [Case 10000]

The "Battle Hymn of the Republic" has come a long way since its beginnings as a Civil War ballad. As it slowly shed its polarizing, Civil War connotations, the song became less of a song from the "North" and more of a song for America. As America moved into the twentieth century, the application of the song continued to evolve. The apocalyptic imagery of war and the language of battle used in the song began to take on a symbolic meaning, thereby allowing the song to be seamlessly applied to any situation of hardship. The song never mentions the Civil War, "North" or "South," or anything that might narrow its applicability. As a result, it has been widely utilized through times of mourning and progress, in literature and movies, in America and abroad.

In response to national tragedies, many artists have performed the "Battle Hymn." The singer Andy

Case 10000 – Item Diagnostics

10001:	*BATTLE HYMN OF THE REPUBLIC AND AVE MARIA*, PERFORMED BY ANDY WILLIAMS Columbia Records Vinyl and paper New York, New York 1968 GC.OBJ.000375.1-.2
10002:	*THE BATTLE HYMN OF THE REPUBLIC*, PERFORMED BY THE MORMON TABERNACLE CHOIR Won the 1959 Grammy Award for Best Pop Performance by a Vocal Group or Chorus Columbia Records Vinyl and paper New York, New York 1959 GC.OBJ.000374.1-.2
10003:	JOHN STEINBECK, *THE GRAPES OF WRATH*, 10TH EDITION Printed by Big Bantham Paper New York, New York September 1955 GC.PBK.002277
10004:	14-CENT JULIA WARD HOWE STAMP, #36 IN THE GREAT AMERICANS SERIES, SHEET OF 100 Paper Boston, Massachusetts February 12, 1987 GC.PPR.010170
10005:	THE THOMPSON CHAIN-REFERENCE BIBLE, OWNED BY JOHNNY CASH Leather and paper United States 1964 GC.BIB.001634

Williams performed it at Robert F. Kennedy's funeral in 1968, after the presidential nominee was assassinated (Item 10001). In 1969, Johnny Cash, whose Bible is on display in this case (Item 10005), sang the song on an episode of his popular television show. At the close of the Cold War, reconciliation between Russia and America was being celebrated in Moscow in 1992, as the Russian Army Chorus performed the "Battle Hymn." The song was not in the program, making it a powerful gesture and a welcome surprise. The hymn was also a cornerstone piece in response to the attacks on September 11, 2001, in both America and England.

Perhaps the Mormon Tabernacle Choir (Item 10002) performed the most famous rendition of the song. In 1959, they signed a record deal with Colombia Records, and their single, "Battle Hymn," sold approximately 300,000 in the first several months. The director of Colombia Records hailed it "a genuine 24 karat hit." The choir's performance won the 1959 Grammy Award for Best Pop Performance by a Vocal Group or Chorus.

The song also permeates literature. John Steinbeck's wife, Carol, suggested the title for 1962 Nobel Prize winner John Steinbeck's realist novel *The Grapes of Wrath* (Item 10003. Steinbeck thought it was a "marvelous" suggestion, and loved that it came from "one of the great songs of the world." Steinbeck, worried that people "might try to give it the communist angle," requested that his publisher include the entire "Battle Hymn" at the beginning of the book. He wrote his publisher saying, "…the Battle Hymn is American and intensely so… So if both words and music are there the book is keyed into the American scene from the beginning." Steinbeck got his wish.

The Original Manuscript of the "Battle Hymn of the Republic"   [Case 10100]

In the darkness of her room at the Willard Hotel, with the voices of Union soldiers bellowing "John Brown's Body" fresh in her mind, Julia Ward Howe composed the first draft of the "Battle Hymn" (Item 10101). In Howe's autobiography, *Reminiscences* (1899), she describes how this manuscript came into being:

> "I awoke in the gray of morning twilight; and as I lay waiting for the dawn, the long lines of the desired poem began to twine themselves in my mind. Having thought out all the stanzas, I said to myself, 'I must get up and write these verses down, lest I fall asleep again and forget them.' So, with a sudden effort, I sprang out of bed, and found in the dimness an old stump of a pen which I remembered to have used the day before. I scrawled the verses almost without looking at the paper. […] At this time, having completed my writing, I returned to bed and fell asleep, saying to myself, 'I like this better than most things that I have written.'"

Throughout her lyrics, Howe calls upon the words of the Bible to capture the images she wishes to portray. The apocalyptic language from verses in the biblical books of Isaiah, Ezekiel, Joel, Daniel, Matthew, and especially the Book of Revelation, enhance the emotion of its lyrical call to "march on." The Bible was widely read in mid-nineteenth century America, as demonstrated by Howe's ability to apply its language organically. One would have been hard-pressed to find an American who did not catch the echoes of Isaiah (6:5) and Revelation (14:19-20) in the opening lines. Similarly, the language used in the fourth stanza, "Let the Hero, born of woman, crush the serpent with His heel," uses imagery from Genesis (3:15) to symbolize defeating an enemy.

Case 10100 – Item Diagnostics

10101:	ORIGINAL DRAFT OF THE BATTLE HYMN OF THE REPUBLIC, WITH COVER LETTER AND ENVELOPE
	"Mine eyes have seen the glory of the coming of the Lord"
	Ink on paper
	Washington, DC
	November 19, 1861
	GC.PPR.010164.1-.3

Although originally written in the context of the Civil War, the style of the symbolism in the song allowed it to be describing a literal battle scene or, instead, an ideological fight for a cause. So, while the song fit well with the Civil War, it also applied to the non-violent fight led by Martin Luther King Jr., who quoted and sang it often. The song's foundation is adaptable. It powerfully expresses emotions that people will inevitably encounter during life, and so, Howe's lyrics and the song "marches on."

Impact Theater—"Book of Books" (Video)

The religious impact of the Bible extends beyond the liturgical practices discussed elsewhere in this section of Passages. An integral part of the Bible's history is the impact it has had in the lives of the wide range of people who have claimed it as their own, and who have used it, not only in their personal lives, but also in every arena of society and culture.

This theatre presents one particular understanding of the Bible's message and impact, as it relates to the religious experience and personal faith of individuals who have chosen to believe its message.

Reprise

Passages: The Bible in Four Movements tells something of the Bible's history, use, and impact in four forceful tracks. More could be said by following other strands or motifs than just these four.

Transmission led us through several modes that the Bible has been broadcast at various times and places. Historically, those who hold the Bible sacred have been early adopters of new media and forms of communication. With the revolution brought by Gutenberg's press technology, the Bible and religious tracts and books became some of the earliest and most popular published. Over the past century, early adoption is seen with new sound and imaging technologies—radio, television, microfiche, sound recording, video recording, live streaming of events, and digital broadcast—both live and recorded—through smart devices. The biblical text has found expression in all of these media. And with the advent of computers and word processors, the religious publishing industry completely confirms the ancient sage's assessment:

"Of making many books there is no end" Ecclesiastes 12:12 (NIV)

All has not been well, though, for the Bible and its users. Dissonance, even destruction, follow its movement through the world, as seen in *Controversy*. With its formation, discordant assessments are heard in both Jewish and Christian communities. Not all books are equally welcome in all communities. Some writings and voices trail off into obscurity with the formalization of the biblical canon. The Protestant Reformation, the Catholic Counter-Reformation, slavery, apartheid, the Spanish Inquisition, the Nazi regime's Holocaust—all sound serious themes of discord and dissonance among those using the Bible as a guide and referent. Desacralization and desecration of the biblical text takes various forms.

In the *Translation* segment, we hear the Bible in many voices through their own tongues and dialects: a deliberate movement, if you will, to reverse the babble of Babel (Genesis 11:1-9), initiated at the first Christian Pentecost (Acts 2), which Christians expect to crescendo in song of "every tribe and language and people and nation" at the end of history (Revelation 5:9 ESV). What some hear as cacophony, others enjoy as harmony, even complex counterpoint. Nonetheless, dissonance has arisen with the Bible's translation into the common tongue, as some religious authorities and political voices suppressed movements they viewed as dangerous. Reviews of "new" translations typically are not kind or favorable, as critics often prefer the older sounds and rhythms they know of the biblical text. Even so, the Bible remains the most translated book of all time, and translation work continues to build and build and build through many groups as more languages and dialects are covered.

Ultimately, as the *Impact* section shows, people encounter the Bible through their own cultures, communities, lives, experiences, and circumstances. Listening to it, some hear one thing, others another. For many, it is music to the mind and heart; for others, its tones are purely discordant.

Amidst all the interweaving themes of this exhibition, still, one thing about the Bible is constant—its significance and importance is found among a great many people throughout history as well as in the world today.

About Museum of the Bible

In the fall of 2017, Museum of the Bible opens its eight floor, 430,000-square-foot museum in Washington, DC.

Museum of the Bible is a place where people can engage with the Bible–its history, narratives, and impact–in their own way through in-depth explorations and interactive media and technologies. The museum and its traveling exhibitions display Ancient Near Eastern, Jewish, and Christian artifacts and documents from the Green Collection. These irreplaceable historical items help tell various stories involving the Bible–as a historical and cultural item as well as a sacred text. The museum seeks to create an atmosphere of wonder and exploration, of reflection and contemplation, inviting all people to look at the Bible anew.

- Museum of the Bible works with some 60 universities and institutions in the study and analysis of artifacts in the Green Collection. The collection aims to create publications for both scholars and the general public, and to endeavor in conservation, imaging, and increasing access to the artifacts for ongoing research, study, and exhibition.
- Museum of the Bible engages in scholarship and academic research with numerous scholars, and in developing mentoring relationships through the Green Scholars Initiative to help train future researchers and scholars of the Bible.
- Museum of the Bible is developing various educational resources, including a high school curriculum about the Bible for both domestic and international use. The curriculum is state-of-the-art and employs convergent media and augmented reality to enhance students' interactive learning experiences.
- As of 2015, Museum of the Bible traveling exhibits have been on display in six U.S. cities and in three other countries: The Vatican, Rome, Italy; Bible Lands Museum Jerusalem, Israel; and S.M.I. Catedral de La Habana, Havana, Cuba. More traveling exhibits are being planned, and new locations sought, to increase access to the museum's artifacts and to invite people to engage with the Bible.

The museum is conveniently located two blocks south of the National Mall and three blocks southwest of the Capitol at the Federal Center SW Metro Station, 300 D Street SW, Washington, DC.

By the Numbers

- Total square footage: 430,000
- Floors: 8 (including underground basement levels)
- Primary, permanent exhibit floors: 5 (Impact, History and Narrative of the Bible; long-term international libraries; and long-term international museum galleries)
- Estimated value of museum's assets on completion: Approximately $800 million
- Workers on-site daily at construction's peak: 500–600

- Number of universities, seminaries and colleges worldwide conducting advanced research on artifacts from the Green Collection: 60
- Floor height (in feet) needed to accommodate exhibits: 25
- Number of cumulative attendees at museum's traveling exhibits since 2011: Well over 500,000
- Biblical garden and restaurant: 1 on rooftop
- Ballroom: Dinner seating for 500, lecture-style seating for 1,000
- Performing arts hall seating capacity: 500
- Number of biblical texts and artifacts on display on the History floor alone: More than 500
- Length in minutes of the *Drive Through History* film on the History floor: 12-15
- Number of blocks from the National Mall: 2
- Number of blocks from the U.S. Capitol: 3

Museum Timeline

- 2009: Green family purchases their first biblical artifact, the Roseberry Rolle manuscript
- 2010: Museum of the Bible established as 501(c)(3) nonprofit
- March 2011: The Green Collection makes public debut to gathering of business, government, academic and religious leaders at the Vatican Embassy in Washington, DC.
- 2011: Green Scholars Initiative partners with University of Oxford (UK) to pioneer multi-spectral imaging technology on manuscripts like the Green Collection's *Codex Climaci Rescriptus*
- May 2011: Traveling exhibit *Passages* premieres at the Oklahoma City Museum of Art; the exhibit later travels to Atlanta; Charlotte, North Carolina; Colorado Springs; Springfield, Missouri; and Santa Clarita, California
- April 2012: *Verbum Domini* ("Word of the Lord") exhibit opens in St. Peter's Square, Vatican City; based upon the success of *Verbum Domini*, a second exhibit, *Verbum Domini II*, opens in March 2014
- July 2012: Washington Design Center purchased for $50 million as site for forthcoming Bible museum
- September 2013: Green Collection purchases world's oldest known Jewish book of prayers (*siddur*); the book of prayers was displayed in Israel for first time in September 2014
- October 2013: *Book of Books* exhibit travels to Bible Lands Museum Jerusalem
- January 2014: *La Biblia* exhibit travels to Havana, Cuba
- Summer 2014: Museum architectural concept submission is approved by the U.S. Commission on Fine Arts, the local DC Advisory Neighborhood Commission and the DC Historic Preservation Review Board; The Terminal Refrigerating and Warehousing Co. building is also designated as an historic landmark by DC's Historic Preservation Review Board

What Others Are Saying

- "A new multimillion-dollar, high-tech, interactive museum of the Bible . . ." (*USA Today*, April 4, 2011)
- "That museum is perhaps as ambitious a project as the collection it will house." (*Philanthropy* magazine, July 1, 2011)
- "Scheduled to open in 2017, the yet-to-be-named museum would welcome people of all faiths and include rare Torahs as well as historic Bibles." (*The New York Times*, July 16, 2014)

- "A museum collection of such great cultural significance will likely be a sought-after destination for the visiting public." (Thomas Luebke, secretary of the U.S. Commission on Fine Arts, *Washington Post Magazine*, Sept. 12, 2014)
- "[T]he [museum's] proposed design had drawn an enthusiastic response from residents because it would rehabilitate the building's imposing exterior and create a new public space." (*The New York Times*, July 16, 2014)
- "The project's cast of leading players...include respected biblical scholars, a deeply religious theme park magnate, and hipster New York designers whose other projects include branding Yankee Stadium and the NBC logo." (*Washington Post Magazine*, Sept. 12, 2014)
- "High-tech museum to take scholarly look at Bible . . . " (*USA Today*, April 4, 2011)

For more information, visit www.museumoftheBible.org.